Knight's Cross Profiles Volume 1

KNIGHT'S CROSS PROFILES

Volume 1

Heinz-Wolfgang Schnaufer • Rudolf Winnerl
Hermann Graf • Hans-Georg Schierholz

Ralf Schumann

Schiffer Military History
Atglen, PA

Book translation by Dr. Edward Force
Book Design by Ian Robertson.

Library of Congress Control Number: 20122931291

This book is a combination of works originally published in German under the series title *Ritterkreuzträger Profile (1-4)* by Flugzeug Publikations GmbH.

Printed in China.
ISBN: 978-0-7643-4057-4

We are interested in hearing from authors with book ideas on related topics.

Published by Schiffer Publishing Ltd.
4880 Lower Valley Road
Atglen, PA 19310
Phone: (610) 593-1777
FAX: (610) 593-2002
E-mail: Info@schifferbooks.com.
Visit our web site at: www.schifferbooks.com
Please write for a free catalog.
This book may be purchased from the publisher.
Try your bookstore first.

In Europe, Schiffer books are distributed by:
Bushwood Books
6 Marksbury Avenue
Kew Gardens
Surrey TW9 4JF, England
Phone: 44 (0) 20 8392-8585
FAX: 44 (0) 20 8392-9876
E-mail: Info@bushwoodbooks.co.uk.
Visit our website at: www.bushwoodbooks.co.uk
Try your bookstore first.

Contents

Heinz-Wolfgang Schnaufer

The Most Successful Night-fighter Pilot of World War II

Decorations:

6/2/1942	Iron Cross 2nd Class
9/9/1942	Iron Cross 1st Class
7/26/1943	Cup of Honor for special accomplishment in air war
8/16/1943	German Cross in gold
12/31/1943	Knight's Cross of the Iron Cross
6/27/1944	507th Oak Leaves to Knight's Cross of the Iron Cross
7/30/1944	84th Swords to Knight's Cross of the Iron Cross
10/16/1944	21st Diamonds to Knight's Cross of the Iron Cross

Promotions:

4/1/1940	Fahnenjunker
4/1/1941	Fahnenjunker-Gefreiter
7/1/1940	Fahnenjunker-Unteroffizier
9/1/1940	Fähnrich
2/1/1941	Oberfähnrich
4/1/1941	Leutnant
7/1/1943	Oberleutnant
5/1/1944	Hauptmann
12/1/1944	Major

Combat Missions:
164

Kills:
121 at night, including 114 four-engine bombers

A Messerschmitt Bf 110 of NJG 1 with black night paint. The beginning of a night mission. By the war's end, some 6150 of the Bf 110 had been built.

On November 15, 1939, Heinz-Wolfgang Schnaufer entered Pilot Training Regiment 42 in Salzwedel. He suspected nothing then of his comet-like career in the Luftwaffe.

"Night fighting—it will never come to that!" Hermann Göring, Kommandeur of the German Luftwaffe, made that assertion in 1939. But he was mistaken, for in 1940 the first enemy missions of British bombers into German territory were made. A new weapon was created: Night fighting, and with it came the night fighter pilots. Just as in daytime combat, aces were to rise from it and become just as renowned as Mölders, Galland, and Marseille.

One of them was Heinz-Wolfgang Schnaufer.

He was the most successful night fighter pilot of World War II. The rudder of his Messerschmitt 110, with markings for 121 kills, can still be seen in the Imperial War Museum in London to this day.

Respectfully dubbed "The Night Ghost" by the British, Heinz-Wolfgang Schnaufer incorporated all the virtüs of a good soldier. For him soldiering was not reflected in blind obedience, but in preparation of details. In discipline and order and in respect for human rights and laws, as well as love for his country. Through the application of his own person, he became a symbol for many young Germans who strove for such ideals toward the end of World War II.

He was the outstanding man of German night fighting. The best flying ability, exemplary tactics, and bold pluck were the decisive elements in a series of successful actions for this extremely brave aerial officer. Night by night he went at the foe, never resting in action against the British bomber fleets, and his combat achievements made him an exemplary symbol of a new service arm, bringing very high sacrifice and gaining high regard, as well as inspiring fear among the enemy through his achievements.

But not just he alone, his crew as well belonged among the best that German night fighting had brought out; a dedicated team in which one had to rely blindly on one another.

Schnaufer took part in 164 missions, scoring twice as many kills at night as the greatest Allied ace, Colonel Ivan Koschedub of the Russian fighter corps, scored by day.

Ralf Schumann

Heinz-Wolfgang Schnaufer was born in Calw, Württemberg, on February 16, 1922, the first son of the engineer and merchant Alfred Schnaufer and his wife, the former Elisabeth Frey, and belonged to that vintage that had to pay an immeasurable price of blood in World War II.

At the age of fourteen he expressed the wish to become an officer. He was able to demonstrate his scholarly and human abilities at, among others, the National Political Training Center (NAPOLA), the successor to the Cadet Academy in the Third Reich. He ranked highest in every school class. Here he won the Reich Youth Sport Medal, the basic certificate of the D.L.R.G., the bronze Hitler Youth Certificate, and passed the B Test in gliding. Before he finished his schooling, he volunteered for the Luftwaffe.

At the age of seventeen, in November 1939, he gained his school diploma with honors as one of the best.

He passed the entrance examination as an officer's aide in the Luftwaffe and entered Pilot Training Regiment 42 in Salzwedel on November 15, 1939. Transferred then to the Training Company of the Aircraft Pilot School (FFS) A/B 3 in Guben, he went through the A/B pilot's license training there by August 20, 1940. This school had its origin in the flight drill center at Guben, northeast of Cottbus. A planned transfer to Sprottau in April 1939, though, was not made, so that as of September 1939 his A/B pilot training took place at the main center in Guben.

During his training as an airplane pilot, the opportunity to fly almost all types of German aircraft was offered to him. Thus, he was trained in the following models: Focke Wulf 44, 56 and 58; Heinkel 72, 41 and 51; Bücker 131; Klemm 35; Arado 66 and 96; Gotha 145; and Junkers types W 34 and 35. From August 1940 to May 1941 he gained the C 3 air pilot's license at the FFS E© in Alt-Loennewitz, near Turgau. There he received outstanding fighter-pilot training, was trained on dive-bombers, and had blind-flying training for fighters and destroyers in lone and group flying at the Blind Flying School 2 in Neuburg, on the Danube. Here the knowledge of how to master the high school of flying–a prerequisite for a pilot's assignment to a combat, long-range reconnaissance, night fighter, or glider unit–was gained.

After finishing his training he was promoted to Leutnant on April 1, 1941.

During his training at the Night Fighter School in Schleissheim, his skills to date were completed through night blind-flying and tactical night-flying training. There he finished his training as a night-fighter pilot in November 1941.

With certification on April 1, 1941, he was promoted to Leutnant and assigned to a front unit. Schnaufer was transferred to the II. Group of Nachtjagdgeschwader (Nachtjagdgeschwader, NJG) 1 and became the technical officer of the unit. This group had developed from the 1. Group of Destroyer Squadron (Zerstörergeschwader, ZG) 76 and had been established in October 1940 as the newly formed II./NJG 1.

NJG 1, though, then at Venlo-Herongen airfield, was to produce the most successful night fighters: names like Helmut Lent (1918-1944), Heinz Strüning (1912-1944), Werner Streib (1911-1986), Günther Radusch (1912-1988), Manfred Meurer (1919-1944), Hans-Joachim Jabs (born 1917), Walter Ehle (1913-1943), and Martin Drewes (born 1918), to name only a few, were closely linked with the success of this squadron and ranked among the elite of their service arm.

Wolfgang Falck (born 1910), at right, set up Nachtjagdgeschwader 1 as of June 26, 1940 and was its first Kommodore. He earned the Knight's Cross October 1, 1940, and commanded the squadron until June 30, 1943. An Oberst at the war's end, Falck then saw service with various staffs in the Luftwaffe. At left in the picture is the later Oak-Leaf bearer and successful night fighter Hermann Greiner.

In mid-January 1942 II./NJG 1 was transferred to St. Trond, Belgium. From there Heinz-Wolfgang Schnaufer's victory parade began; at that time he was still an unknown twenty-year-old Leutnant in the German Luftwaffe.

During the night of June 1-2, 1942, on his 13th mission, he scored his first night kill on a four-engine British Handley-Page "Halifax" heavy bomber near Grenz-Donau, 15 kilometers from Louvain. But in his attempt to shoot down a second bomber, Schnaufer was struck in the left thigh by an anti-aircraft shot at the start of the attack. The plane—his "Dora-Cäsar"—had taken 19 hits, which resulted in one rudder failing because a cable duct was shot through; the left engine was on fire and the spotlight, damaged from the enemy fire, would not turn off. So Schnaufer had to break off the attack and return to St. Trond.

His patience had been rewarded and he had scored his first kill, for which he and his radioman (bordfunker) Rumpelhardt were awarded the Iron Cross Second Class.

Schnaufer hoped that the bullet in his left thigh would encapsulate and he could go on flying missions, but on 8 June he was sent to a hospital in Brussels.

Recovered again, he was able to shoot down five more enemies within a short time, which was recognized in his decoration with the Iron Cross First Class on September 9, 1942. He had shot down Handley-Page "Halifax", Vickers "Wellington", and Armstrong Whitworth "Whitley" bombers.

Schnaufer had scored seven kills by the end of 1942 and begun to become an ace in his craft.

But familiarity and experience with his plane could not alone account for his success and return from a night mission. Along with the nerve-wracking problems of spotting an enemy in the darkness came the danger from the alert British gunners. Sometimes the German night fighters were spotted by them before they had been seen. There were also the defensive weapons manned by the planes' gunners, weapon mounts with coupled machine guns, and later even heavier guns that allowed the night fighters to be attacked before they could get into attack positions. The gunners had a task of spotting the night fighters and shooting them down as quickly as possible. The gunners also knew they were fighting for their lives, since they were the first to have machine-gun bursts aimed at them from the night fighters. German survivors still hold great respect for the Royal Air Force gunners to this day.

General Josef Kammhuber, Kommandeur of the 1st Night Fighter Division. He organized the night fighters and created bright night fighting, the canopy process, and the Kammhuber Bolt.

Their own anti-aircraft fire was also a danger. In many cases German night fighters were shot down by their own side, while others fell to the British night fighters, who also knew their craft and escorted the bomber packs. The British night fighters, equipped at first with the Bristol "Beaufighter" and later with the faster, more agile "Mosquito", were an unpleasant disturbance for the German night-fighter crews. The German pilots paid a high price in physical and nervous systems while taking off, flying, and landing at night. These constant dangers made the night-fighters' work some of the most demanding in World War II.

In the summer months of 1943 Schnaufer's climb to the highest rank of night-fighter aces began. On the night of May 29-30, 1943, he shot down three enemies (10th and 11th air kills).

On July 26, 1943, he was awarded the Cup of Honor for special achievement in air warfare, and on August 16, 1943, he was decorated with the German Cross in gold.

The creators of German night fighting, from left to right: Werner Streib, here as Hauptmann and Kommandeur of I./NJG 1, Major Wolfgang Falck, Kommodore of NJG 1, and Generalmajor Josef Kammhuber.

Leutnant Schnaufer, a still-unknown beginner in night fighting, gets into his Me 110.

Schnaufer prepares for one of his first missions with NJG 1 and closes his plane's canopy. No one knew then that he would become the most successful night fighter of all times and nations.

Three more kills, the 15th to 17th, followed on the night of June 28-29, 1943. His twentieth kill was scored on the night of July 8-9, 1943, and his thirtieth on October 8-9, 1943. The outstanding event of the year was the victory over four enemies in one night on December 16-17, 1943, which brought his score up to 40 kills.

Schnaufer felt called more and more to fighting, and requested to be released as a technical officer and named the leader of a squadron. His superior officers had recognized his abilities for some time. At that time he was transferred to night fighting and his wish was fulfilled.

A squad captain as of August 1943 in the most successful German night-fighter group, IV./NJG 1, he now led the 12.Staffel, based at Quakenbrück. To date he had been able to score 21 kills. His Gruppenkommandeur was Hauptmann Hans-Joachim Jabs.

On Novemver 27, 1943, at 6:07 P.M., Schnaufer took off from Leeuwarden, where he had recently moved for Zahme Sau ("Tame Boar") action against an expected stream of bombers. His decision to attack the enemy planes from there proved to be right. By 6:50 P.M. and again at 7:00 he shot down planes northwest of Meppen and northwest of Cloppenburg. He landed back at Quakenbrück at 7:40 P.M.

By December 16, 1943, he was able to raise his score to 36 kills. On 29 December he took off in bad weather in the "Polar Bear" area, where he was able to shoot down a Handley-Page "Halifax" near Dijkhuizen and an Avro "Lancaster" near Lingen.

After a total of 42 kills, he was decorated with the Knight's Cross of the Iron Cross on December 31, 1943, at the rank of Oberleutnant.

From now on, scarcely a night's action took place from which he did not return with one or more aerial victories. From then on, a series of unending victories continued. On 27 and 30 January he scored two more kills.

His fiftieth score on the night of February 15-16, 1943, in which he overcame three enemies, was also the group's 500th aerial victory, which was celebrated appropriately.

On March 17, 1944, IV./NJG 1 was transferred back to St. Trond, Belgium.

By May 1, 1944, Schnaufer had been able to shoot down 61 enemy planes.

On the night of May 25, 1944, he shot down five Avro "Lancasters" within fourteen minutes. His stellar career continued nonstop.

On the night of June 16-17, 1944, he was able to shoot down his 79th and 80th enemy planes. Just seven days later he celebrated his 84th success.

After this 84th kill, he became the German Wehrmacht's 507th soldier to be decorated with the Oak Leaves of the Knight's Cross.

Barely a month later, after his 87th to 89th kills on July 28-29, 1944, he became the 84th soldier to receive the swords to the Oak Leaves, given directly by Adolf Hitler on August 2, 1944, when he visited the Führer's headquarters to receive the Oak Leaves.

The action did not leave Schnaufer unmarked. Visibly tired and with dark rims under his eyes, he flew his first missions as Technical Officer of NJG 1.

Schnaufer now stood at the zenith of German night fighters. Only Major Helmut Lent, who was awarded the 32nd swords on August 2, 1943, after 93 night kills, and Hauptmann Heinrich Prince of Sayn-Wittgenstein (1916-1944), who was to become the 44th Wehrmacht soldier to receive the Swords when he died, had scored more kills than he.

On August 13, 1943, he scored another series of four kills within 31 minutes.

On March 1, 1944, he took command of IV./NJG 1 in St. Trond, Belgium, replacing Major Jabs, who now succeeded Werner Streib as Squadron Kommodore. On May 1, 1944, he was promoted to Hauptmann. Streib was named inspector of the Night Fighters.

Filled with the unquenchable desire to see action, he scored one success after another, even at a time when the star of German night fighting began to dim.

His iron nerve, the overwhelming quality of always finding new ways to attack enemy bombers, and his lightning fast reaction time made him not only an ace, but also an example to the group he led, which under his leadership had scored over 700 night kills.

As of the spring of 1941, the so-called "canopy process", with one Freya early warning radar set (above) and two Würzburg devices (below) each, operated to locate enemy planes, formed a belt of positions for precise direction of night fighters. At the air traffic headquarters the arriving information was combined. Enemy and German planes were made visible by lights on a card table, and thus the German planes, via special radio signals, could be directed at the enemy.

The equipment of the Bf 110 night fighter was constantly improved throughout its use, so that long-term problems involving the short range of the SN-2 device could be solved and the Bf 110 could remove the single-pole A-1 antenna.

On June 12, 1944, Schnaufer shot down three Avro "Lancaster" bombers within seven minutes at an altitude of only 1000 to 1500 meters near Cambrai, France. After landing in St. Trond, the armorers found that for all three kills with two MK 108 machine cannons only 18 shells had been fired. This may well have been an unequaled record.

In a bomb attack on Lille on June 16, 1944, Heinz-Wolfgang Schnaufer attained his 75th aerial victory near Arras.

The crew scored four kills on June 22, 1944, three of them within eleven minutes while flying at 5000 to 5200 meters between Eindhoven and Maastricht, while the fourth came on its exit from German air space at only 2900 meters.

The British intelligence service was very well informed about this man who, night after night, shot down one plane after another from its streams of bombers. All efforts to put him or his group out of action failed. The British High Command sent De Haviland "Mosquito" MK II night fighters to fire on him, and they sent De Haviland "Mosquito" MK VI high-speed bombers ahead of the bomber streams; they were supposed to shower the St. Trond airfield with bombs and make it impossible for his group to take-off. Nothing helped. Schnaufer always found a way to attack the bombers and continued to shoot down one enemy bomber after another.

The British Marshal of the Royal Air Force, Sir Arthur Traves Harris, known as "Bomber Harris". He led the night attacks of British bomber units against German cities and industrial targets. He served in the Air Ministry from 1940 to 1942 and, as of February 1942, as commander of the RAF Bomber Command, being partly responsible for the forced air war (surface bombardment) against Germany, particularly against the civilian population.

A British Armstrong Whitworth "Whitley" bomber. Planes of this type, powered by two Rolls-Royce Merlin X 12-cylinder engines, saw action from 1939 to 1944, and were the first bombers to fly over Berlin. They had five-man crews and a range of 2400 km, were armed with five 7.7 mm machine guns, and could carry a bomb load of 3180 kg.

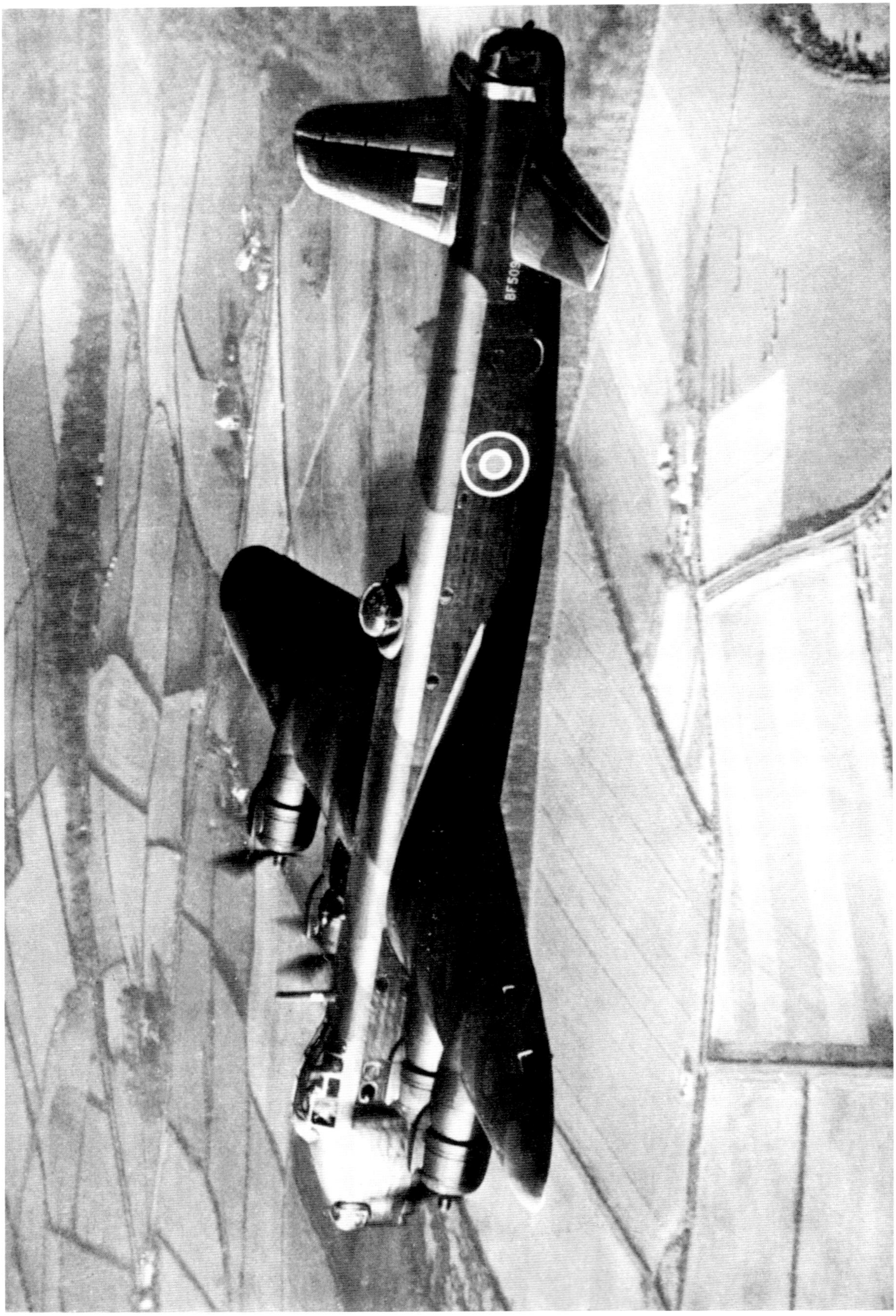

The "Short Stirling" was the first four-engine Allied bomber, and flew night missions against German targets until 1943. Powered by four 1590 HP Bristol Hercules XI double-star engines, it had a crew of seven or eight men, a range of 3090 km, a top speed of 416 kph, and carried a bomb load of 6350 kg and eight 7.7 mm Browning machine guns.

On July 1, 1943, the Kommandeur of I./NJG 1, Werner Streib (1911-1986), became Kommodore of NJG 1. A destroyer pilot when the war began, he scored the first official German night kills on the night of July 19-20, 1940, and helped night fighting break through with his further success in the ensuing months. On October 6, 1940, he received the Knight's Cross, on February 26, 1943, the 197th Oak Leaves, and on March 11, 1944, the 54th Swords. Streib ended the war as Oberst and Inspector of Night Fighters. On some 150 missions he was able to shoot down 67 planes by night and one by day. He can rightfully be called the "spiritus rector" of the German night fighters.

In July 1943 the RAF began to use so-called "window" in a series of effective attacks on Hamburg. It consisted of billions of small strips of reflective metal foil tuned to the wave length of the German C-1 radar. The night fighters were disturbed by it, which resulted in fewer kills. After that the Bf 110 G-4b was equipped with the Lichtenstein SN-2 device, which tuned out this disturbance by using a different wave length.

At the beginning of September 1944 the group moved to Dortmund-Brakel. Once again Schnaufer was able to score four kills within 32 minutes on 23 September, this time over the border area on the Arnheim-Rhine Heights.

On five nights in a row he shot four four-engine planes down. On the night of 9-10 October he scored his 100th kill.

Then, on October 16, 1944, he became the 21st soldier of the German Wehrmacht and the 11th member of the Luftwaffe to be awarded the Diamonds to the Oak Leaves and Swords. Heinz-Wolfgang Schnaufer was the ninth Luftwaffe member of the flying groups and the second night fighter, after Colonel Helmut Lent, who received this high honor.

On October 18, 1944, the General Command of I.Jagdkorps issued the following corps order:

"*The Führer and Supreme Kommandeur of the Wehrmacht has awarded Hauptmann Schnaufer, Kommandeur of IV./NJG 1, as the 21st soldier of the German Wehrmacht, the*

OAK LEAVES WITH SWORDS AND DIAMONDS
TO THE KNIGHT'S CROSS OF THE IRON CROSS.

In a stormy course of victories, borne with the highest fighting spirit, Hauptmann Schnaufer has scored success on success in high multiple aerial victories during a single night mission. The attaining of 100 night-fighter kills, among which victories over 92 large enemy combat aircraft are included, has now led to the awarding of this highest German war decoration. I congratulate Hauptmann Schnaufer in grateful recognition of his undying heroic service and extend to him and his proven crew, Knight's Cross bearers Leutnant Rumpelhardt and Oberfeldwebel Gänsler, my fullest recognition. The entire I. Jagdkorps looks with proud joy upon Hauptmann Schnaufer today."

(signed) Schmid"

On the night of November 6-7, 1944, within fifteen minutes in the time from 7:26 to 7:41 P.M., Schnaufer shot down three more Avro "Lancaster" bombers and thus recorded his 101st to 103rd aerial victories.

The Crew

But this success cannot be attributed to him alone.

His crew, the sworn and experienced team of the Me 110, which had a significant share in this success, consisted of the bordunker Friedrich Rumpelhardt and gunner (bordschützen) Wilhelm Gänsler.

Radioman Friedrich Rumpelhardt

Friedrich Rumpelhardt was born on June 19, 1920, in Nordhalden, near Constance on Lake Constance. Since July 1941 he had flown with Heinz-Wolfgang Schnaufer, at first at the Destroyer School in Wunsiedel, then at the Night Fighter School in Schleissheim. In November 1941 they both joined the 5th Staffel of Nachtjagdgeschwader 1, where Rumpelhardt was promoted to Unteroffizier. He accompanied his plane leader on his steep course to become the most successful night fighter over the II. Group of Nachtjagdgeschwader 1, the 12th Staffel of the Geschwaders, its staff, and the staff of Nachtjagdgeschwader 4.

On October 1, 1943, Rumpelhardt was promoted to Fahnenjunker-Feldwebel and trained to be an officer at the War School. His promotion to Leutnant took place on March 1, 1944, and he was also Intelligence Officer of the Group and Geschwaderstab.

On March 20, 1944, he was honored with the trophy for outstanding achievement in aerial war, and on April 16, 1944, he was decorated with the German Cross in Gold. For taking part in 68 night-fighter kills he was awarded the Knight's Cross on August 8, 1944.

On March 7, 1945, he celebrated his 100th participation, and on March 8, 1945, he was awarded the Oak Leaves to the Knight's Cross. The most successful bordfunker of the German night fighters flew his last combat mission on April 9, 1945.

In the period from May 14 to October 3, 1943, Friedrich Rumpelhardt took various courses of study. During this time Heinz-Wolfgang Schnaufer scored 21 kills with the following gunners:

- 12 with Leutnant Dr. Leo Baro,
- 5 with Oberfeldwebel Erich Handke (Knight's Cross July 27, 1944),
- 2 with Oberleutnant Freymann, and
- 2 with Unteroffizier Bärwolf.

Rumpelhardt took off as Heinz-Wolfgang Schnaufer's bordfunker 123 times, 119 of them with combat missions and four times with other targets. In all there were 44 successful

The wreckage of a shot-down "Wellington" bomber.

Reichsmarschall Göring visits NJG 1 in the autumn of 1943. To the left of him is General Kammhuber; in the center, with the Knight's Cross, is Kommodore Oberstleutnant Streib.

To the joy of all, Göring is reported to by successful crews, including that of Knight's Cross bearer Meurer, seen here.

Earnest faces during the Reichsmarschall's speech. Next to Hauptmann Jabs (Knight's Cross on October 1, 1940, 430th Oak Leaves on March 24, 1944), Kommandeur of IV./NJG 1, are Oberleutnant Schnaufer, already a bearer of the German Cross in Gold, Oberleutnant Drewes (Knight's Cross on July 27, 1944, 839th Oak Leaves on April 17, 1945), and Oberfeldwebel Vinke (Knight's Cross on September 19, 1943, 465th Oak Leaves on April 25, 1944).

The Avro "Lancaster", here a Mark II, reached the troops early in 1942 and flew its first air raid in March of that year. With a range of 2660 km and a bomb load of up to 6350 kg, the "Lancaster" was the most renowned bomber of the British Bomber Command. On the night of May 17, 1943, Lancasters flew, among others, raids on the Moehne, Eder, and Sorpe dams and destroyed them later. On November 12, 1944, "Lancaster" bombers sank the German battleship Tirpitz in Tromso Fjord. Fitted with four 12-cylinder Rolls-Royce Merlin engines, the "Lancaster" reached a top speed of up to 460 kph. Armed with Browning 303 machine guns and with a seven-man crew, these planes, 7374 of which were built, were among the bombers constantly over Germany by night.

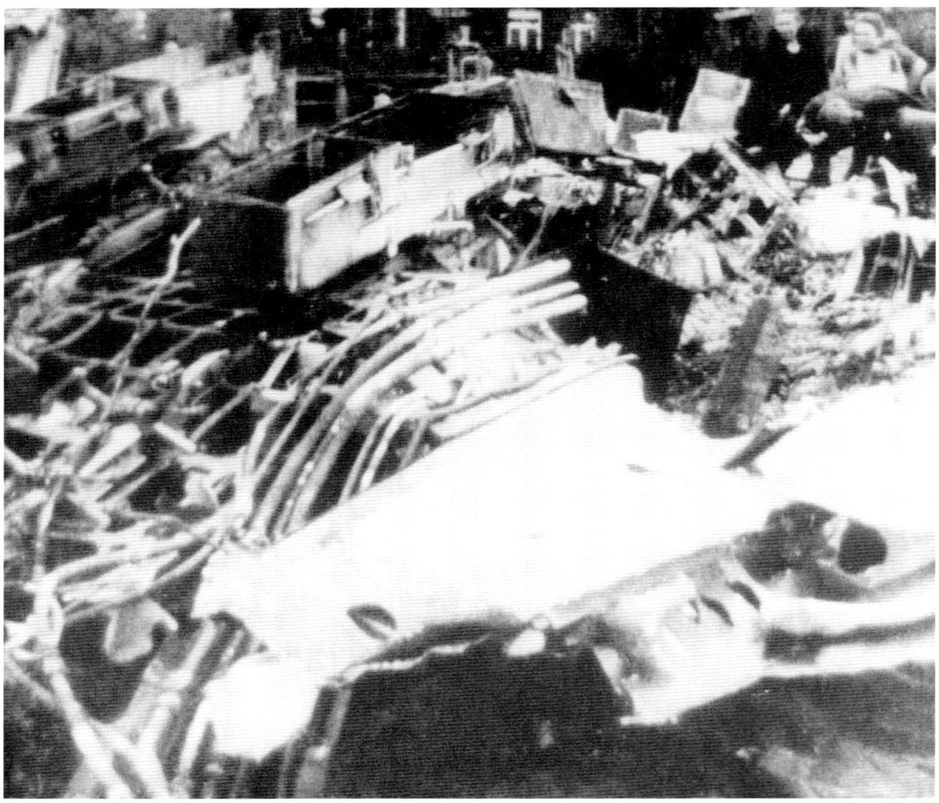

On October 22, 1943, Schnaufer shot down this Lancaster on the return flight from a raid on Kassel, in the vicinity of Höxter.

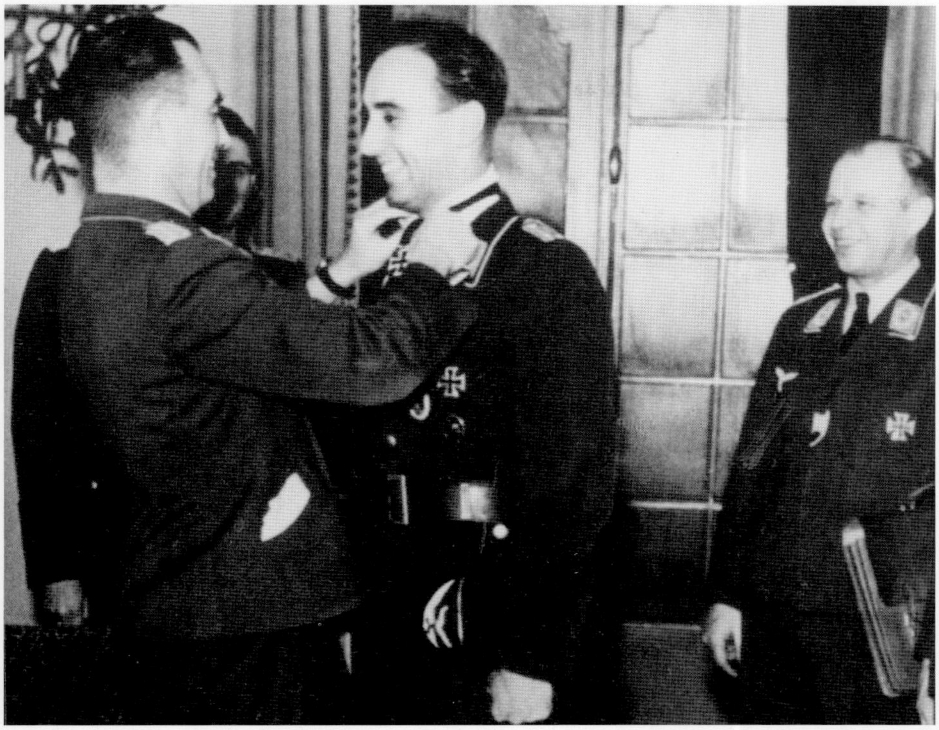

On January 3, 1944, Generalmajor Joseph Schmid, General Kammhuber's successor as Commanding General of the XII. Flying Corps, decorates Oberleutnant Schnaufer with the Knight's Cross awarded on December 31, 1943.

missions: 14 of them with one kill, 15 with two, eight with three, five with four, one with five, and one with seven kills. His flight book registers a total of 636 flights, 119 training flights, in wartime. He flew with Heinz-Wolfgang Schnaufer a total of 549 times.

Bordschütze Wilhelm Gänsler

Wilhelm Gänsler, the gunner in Schnaufer's crew, was born on May 22, 1919, in Arnstadt, Thuringia. He attended public school and completed training as a machinist. Then he volunteered for the Luftwaffe and passed the test for acceptance as an aspiring pilot. After completing his Reich work service, he was sworn into the Luftwaffe in Stade in 1938. In the spring of 1941 Gänsler joined the 4th Staffel of Nachtjagdgeschwader 1 and flew from November 1, 1941, to the summer of 1942 as the gunner in a Dornier Do 215 in the crew of Ludwig Becker (1911-1943).

Hauptmann Becker, likewise an experienced night-fighting ace, received the Oak Leaves to his Knight's Cross on February 26, 1943, after shooting down 44 enemy planes. On the same day he fell in daytime action against American bombers over the North Sea. His radioman, Sergeant-Major Straub, was lost with him.

Gänsler, who now belonged to Schnaufer's crew, in which he was to remain until the war ended, was famous for his excellent vision.

The first official photo after the awarding of the Knight's Cross.

Named Staffelkapitän of 12./NJG 1, Schnaufer had to take on unpleasant duties. Here he speaks the last words at the graves of Leutnant Rühle's crew.

His ability gained appropriate recognition in the awarding of the trophy of honor for outstanding achievement in the air war on January 17, 1944, and of the German Cross in Gold on March 20, 1944. Just like Rumpelhardt, he followed his plane leader through all the steps of his military and aviation career.

After taking part in shooting down 80 planes, Oberfeldwebel Wilhelm Gänsler was decorated with the Knight's Cross of the Iron Cross on July 27, 1944. In over 150 combat missions, he was able to participate in 115 night kills: 17 credited to Ludwig Becker and 98 to that of Heinz-Wolfgang Schnaufer. On March 8, 1945, he was also awarded the Oak Leaves.

British Handley Page Halifax bombers, here Mark II Series I models, more and more of which reached the bomber commands from 1940 on and flew night missions over Germany and France. These four-engine planes had seven-man crews and could carry a 5900-kg bomb load.

Schnaufer, Staffelkapitän of 12./NJG 1, talks with a crew that has returned from a mission.

After the war he returned to his home in Thuringia, but did not find good living or working conditions there. In 1949 Heinz-Wolfgang Schnaufer set him up in his father's business. He was retained there after Schnaufer's death and the employees were made available to expand the enterprise until he retired.

Wilhelm Gänsler, the most successful radioman of the German night fighters, died on November 22, 1985, in Calw, Württemberg, Heinz-Wolfgang Schnaufer's birthplace.

Promotion to Kommodore

On November 20, 1944, Heinz-Wolfgang Schnaufer was named Kommodore of Nachtjagdgeschwader 4, stationed in Gütersloh, It had been established on May 1, 1942, at first with the task of protecting southern Germany from the large-scale night air raids that were beginning then. He was also promoted to Major effective December 1, 1944. Thus he became a Staffelkapitän at the age of twenty-two.

Along with the squadron staff, II/ Group was stationed there. The I. Group was at Frankfurt Rhein-Main Airport and the III. Group in Kassel-Rothwesten.

The staff consisted, besides Schnaufer, of Oberleutnant Eberhardt Koltermann as Adjutant, Leutnant Falk von Tettenborn as Technical Officer, and Friedrich Rumpelhardt as Radio Intelligence Officer. Gruppenkommandeurs were Hauptmann Hubert Rauh of I. Group and Hauptmann Kurt Fladrich of III. Group. With these officers, Schnaufer had experienced night-fighter pilots at his side. In the spring of 1945 Rauh and Fladrich were to receive the Knight's Cross.

On November 22, 1944, Schnaufer and his crew flew from Gütersloh to the Dortmund area on their first mission, and at once scored two victories.

On November 27, 1944, the Schnaufer crew flew to Berlin-Staaken, where Schnaufer was awarded the Diamonds by Hitler. After a photo shoot by Hitler's photographer Heinrich Hoffmann, and a visit to Colonel von Below, Hitler's personal Luftwaffe Adjutant in the Reich Air Ministry, where among other things, a film of the crew was made and later shown in weekly newsreels, the crew had a small party and returned to Gütersloh the third day.

The rudder of Schnaufer's Me 110 is adorned with 46 kill markings. From left to right: Leutnant Matzak, Leutnant Rolland, Schnaufer, and Oberleutnant Weissflog (Knight's Cross on June 24, 1944).

Ready for the next mission, Schnaufer gives a friendly wave to his comrades, confident of victory.

The "Night Ghost" of St. Trond prepares for a new mission.

A British bomber of the Vickers Armstrong "Wellington" Mark IC type. Used for night missions from September 1939 on, the "Wellington" was among the most notable planes of World War II. Powered by two 1585 HP Bristol Hercules VI double-star engines, which gave it a top speed of 408 kph, the "Wellington", thanks to its geodetic structure, could bear great shot damage. It carried a six-man crew and up to 2720 kg of bombs. "Wellington" bombers flew the war's first air raid on Wilhelmshaven on September 4, 1939. From September 1939 to the advent of the heavy bombers, it was the RAF's most important night bomber.

Serious expressions for Kommodore Streib (center), his Intelligence Officer Weissflog (left), and the Staffelkapitän of the 12./NJG 1, Heinz-Wolfgang Schnaufer.

Bottom left: Oberstleutnant Lent, Kommodore of NJG 3, visits IV./NJG 1 in St. Trond, Belgium.

Bottom right: Lent and Schnaufer, now leaving IV./NJG 1 as its Kommandeur, have a serious talk.

Second from right is Wilhelm Gänsler, gunner in Hauptmann Schnaufer's crew.

But when he took over as Kommodore of the squadron, his areas of tasks and responsibility also changed; thus Schnaufer could not fly every night. Yet when the tasks of a Squadron Kommodore allowed, he flew further missions against the numerically superior bombers. Thus he could inspire the individual crews of the squadron, hold task discussions, and deal with paperwork.

With this position, though, Schnaufer fulfilled his wish to fly the Me 110 with the four upward-pointing 2 cm guns, later known as "Slanted Music", on his own missions. Now he could fly below the bomber packs and attack them without being seen. On his own initiative he had such a plane assembled, and flew his first mission with it shortly thereafter. The effect was astounding; after the first bursts of fire Schnaufer had scored his kills without being seen by the enemy.

With his 106th kill on December 12-13, 1944, he ranked at the head of the night fighters. Thus Heinz-Wolfgang Schnaufer had exceeded the achievements of the formerly leading German night fighter, Oberstleutnant Helmut Lent.

Lent, who had been the first night fighter and 15th soldier of the German Wehrmacht to receive the Diamonds to the Knight's Cross with Oak Leaves and Swords on July 31, 1944, after the 102nd of his 105 kills, including eight on one day, crashed while landing at Paderborn during a daylight transfer flight on 7 October and died in hospital of his wounds on October 11, 1944. Lent was posthumously promoted to Oberst. His longtime radioman, Knight's Cross bearer Walter Kubisch (born 1918), also lost his life. Thus Heinz-Wolfgang Schnaufer became his heir as the most successful German night fighter.

Leutnant Helmut Lent, member of NJG 1 from September 1940 to November 1941, was the most successful German night fighter until his death. After his 102nd night kill, he was the first night fighter and 15th Wehrmacht soldier to receive the diamonds. In all he scored 113 aerial victories, including eight in one day. He was promoted to Oberst posthumously.

Hauptmann Schnaufer, ready for his next mission, is belted in by his first assistant, N.C.O. Ulrich.

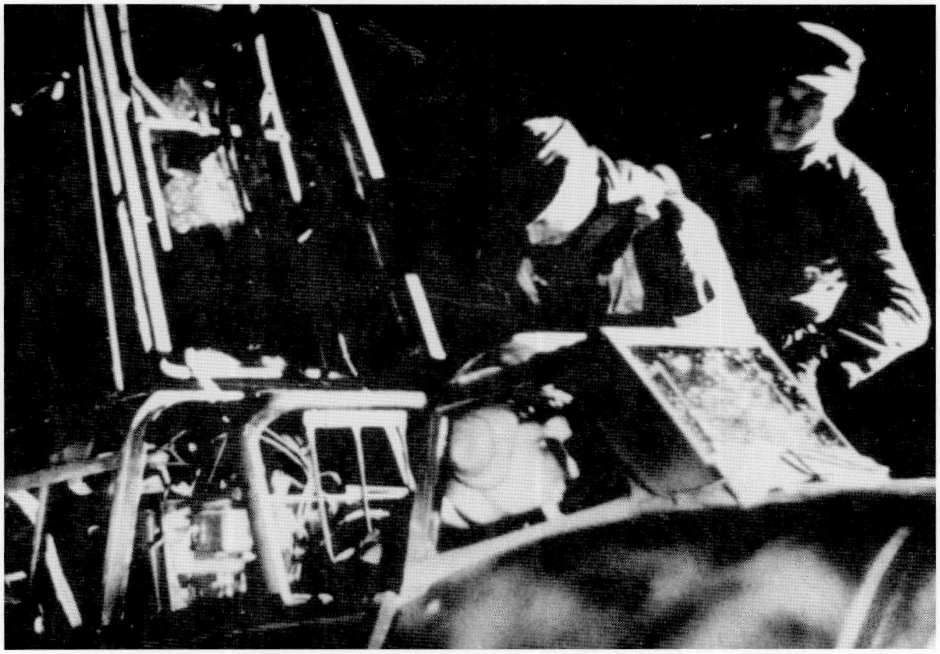

Leutnant Rumpelhardt, radioman in the Schnaufer crew, prepares to come aboard.

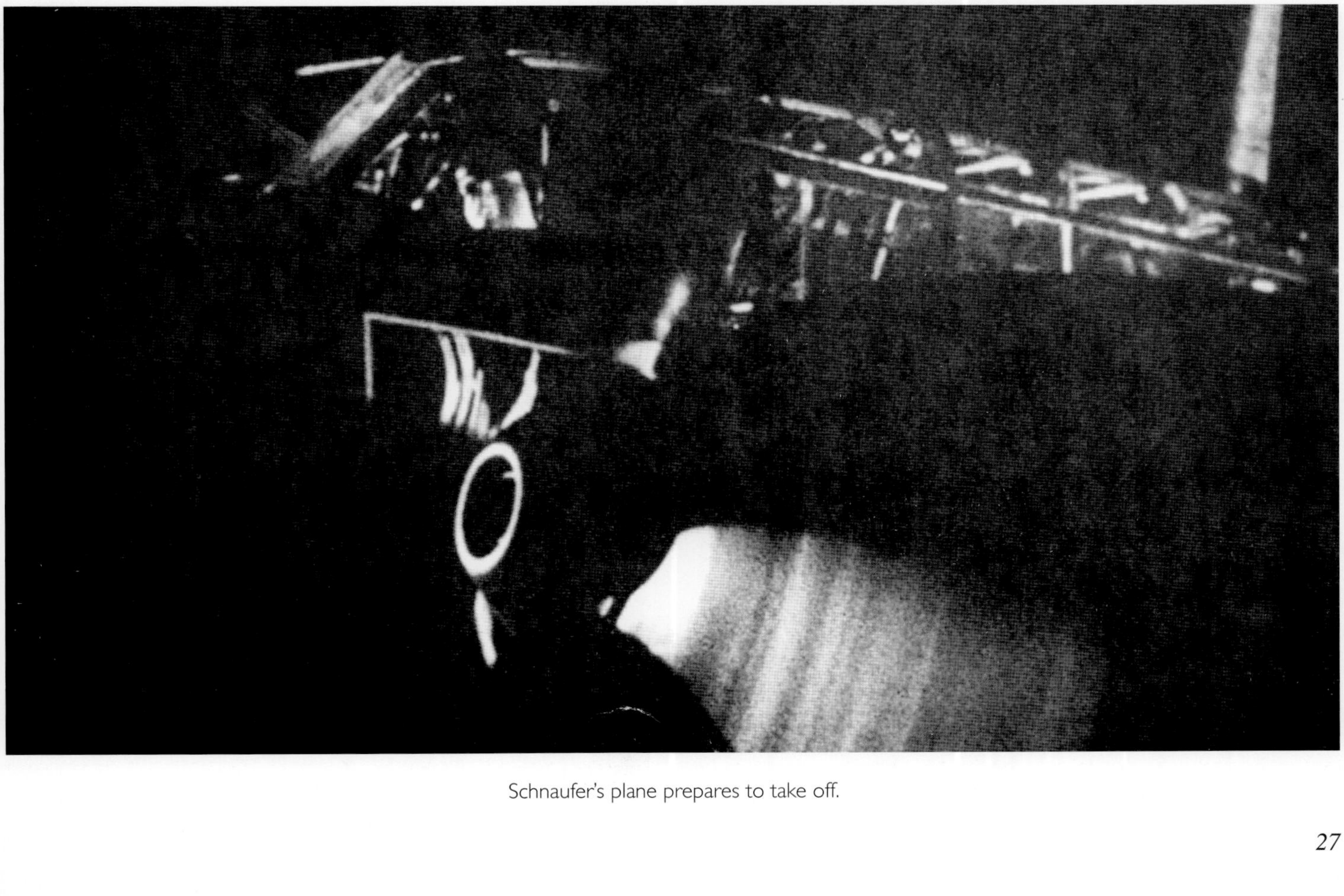

Schnaufer's plane prepares to take off.

Generalmajor Walter Grabmann (1905-1992), Kommandeur of the 3rd Fighter Division since November 7, 1943, visits NJG 1 at St. Trond. Grabman received the Knight's Cross on September 14, 1940, and was Fighter-Pilot Leader and Division Kommandeur in the Reich's defense as of August 1942. As of April 1, 1945, he commanded the 1st Fighter Division.

On February 8, 1945, Heinz-Wolfgang Schnaufer was summoned to "Karinhall", the headquarters of the Reichsmarschall, who had announced his intention of appointing Schnaufer Inspector of the Night Fighters. At that time Colonel Streib held that position. But Schnaufer declined this promotion, as it was against his nature to push one of his best friends and mentors out of the position. Schnaufer, who thus made his refusal known, saying that he wanted to continue to apply his knowledge and all his ability in action, was able to persuade Göring to leave him in his present position.

On February 16, 1945, his 23rd birthday, he received a very special honor. While listening to the radio in the officers' home, another officer had turned on the forbidden Calais army station, and the British wished him a happy birthday. The voice, which spoke fluent German, spoke directly to the soldiers of NJG 4 in Gütersloh. Shortly thereafter, the voice praised the Kommodore as the world's best and most successful night fighter, and congratulated him on his birthday, calling his actions fair and recognizing him as a respected opponent. After that a dance band played the song "The Night Ghost, the Night Ghost, walks in our castle" as a song of praise, giving him the title of "Night Ghost" of St. Trond from the British bomber crews. Schnaufer himself did not hear the radio broadcast, but comrades told him of it.

Meanwhile, his score of successful missions continued. On the night of February 21-22, 1945, he was able to crown his career by shooting down eight Avro "Lancaster" bombers within 26 minutes, scoring his 110th to 116th kills. In a second action he shot down two more bombers, raised his score to 118, and thus shot down a whole squad of British bombers alone in one night.

After he scored his 119th to 121st aerial victories on March 7-8, 1945, he was forbidden to fly. His experience and ability were not to be put at risk. Those were his last victories.

In March 1945, on orders from the High Command, he tested the Dornier 335 for night use. His last mission took place on April 9, 1945. Taking off from Fassberg at 10:00 P.M., he landed 79 minutes later at 11:19 P.M. He had tried in vain to attack an Avro "Lancaster" that was heavily protected.

The Kommodore, Major Jabs, visits IV. Group of NJG 1 and is greeted by Gruppenkommandeur Schnaufer.

The Castle of St. Trond, housing for the elite of the German night fighters.

The St. Trond airfield, Belgium, by day. Between missions, necessary servicing work was done to the planes.

Summer 1944 at St. Trond, from left to right: Generalmajor Grabmann (Kommandeur of the 3rd Fighter Division), Schnaufer and Jabs.

Night-fighter crews spend time between missions playing cards.

On April 11, 1945, Schnaufer took over the defense of the Eggeberg field, about halfway between Schleswig and Flensburg, to defend the transfer of part of the squadron to Fassberg. Barracks in the town of Bolingstedt, some 5 km from the field, offered lodging to the crews. On April 13, 1945, almost all the planes were destroyed or damaged by fighter-bombers. The Hungarian anti-aircraft troops were undefended against the rolling attacks. Schnaufer's "BA" was fully destroyed. As the only crew of the squadron, he still flew the Bf 110. After a short time G9+DX was flown to him by the Kommodore of NJG 1, Leutnant Colonel Jabs, and he flew it on his last mission on the night of April 19-20, 1945, with the squadron's only crew.

When the war ended, Major Heinz-Wolfgang Schnaufer gave his last daily order to NJG 4. With this document the ace of aces among the night fighters expressed all that was still to be said:

To my tried and true NJG 4

Command post, May 8, 1945

Men of my Squadron!

The enemy is in our land, our proud airplanes are surrendered. Germany is occupied and has capitulated unconditionally.

The Lichtenstein SN-2 antennas of the later Bf 110G-AC were mounted at an angle to improve their reception. The gun mounts for the 20 mm caliber MG 151 and 30 mm caliber MK 108 can be seen clearly.

The Fu 212 "Lichtenstein" radar.

The De Havilland "Mosquito". Used as a night fighter and fitted with A.I. radar, the Mosquito was feared by the German night-fighter crews. At first the British night-fighter groups still used the Bristol "Beaufighter", later being supplied with the faster and more agile "Mosquito". The British High Command sent De Havilland "Mosquito" Mark II night fighters to shoot down Heinz-Wolfgang Schnaufer, while De Havilland "Mosquito" Mark VI fast bombers were sent to precede the bomber packs and bomb the St. Trond airfield to make it impossible for Schnaufer and his crews to take off. With a top speed of up to 635 kph, the lightly built "Mosquito" was powered by two Rolls-Royce Merlin 12-cylinder engines producing up to 1635 HP. From 1940 to the war's end, 6710 of them were built.

"Christmas trees," glowing markers ejected by British pathfinder planes that preceded the bomber packs, marked the attack targets onto which the following bombers dropped their deadly loads.

Comrades, this depressing fact brings tears to our eyes. The future lies before us, unknowable and undeniable, it can bring us only sorrow and pain.

But something will always live on in us, my men—the tradition of our squadron and our achievements. This tradition will give us the strength we need when we are abased, it will straighten our backs and let us look into the future with pride.

Once again I want to call back to your minds the history of our renowned squadron, feared by the enemy. Just three years ago, on May 1, 1942, the NJG 4 Squadron was founded and, at first, given the task of defending southern Germany from the beginning large-scale night raids. Mainz-Fintheim, Laupheim, Jovincourt and Laon-Athies were our first bases, then in 1943 Florennes, St. Dizier and Coulommieres.

But we did not need to define our development only by empty names. There where we rose night after night, the soil of France and southern Germany is covered by many small scars from the pyres of the big bombers we shot down.

579 bombers, three complete bomber divisions, were shot down by NJG 4 in tough air battles under the hardest conditions.

Successful night missions in all weather against Avranches, Nijwegen, vehicle columns and rail lines in the backlands have cost the enemy hundreds of vehicles and locomotives. Thus the names of "Wild Bird" and "Whirlwind" sound good to us.

Long-distance raids over Britain were among our squadron's last strikes. The destruction of the pontoon bridges at Wesel meant for us the renowned conclusion of our renowned hard fight.

Comrades, these great achievements were gained only through your unshakable steadfastness, your energy and your faith in Germany.

Through the hard blows of the enemy air forces, we were often not far from being crushed by their overwhelming material strength, but we have struck back in a cold fury until the end.

A British bomber, shot down by a German night fighter, goes down in flames.

Well camouflaged, the planes stand at the edge of the airfield by day. This plane has Rüstsatz (Equipment Set) 3, with four forward-firing MG 17 machine guns replaced by two MK 108 30 mm cannons.

This unequal battle has cost us the most serious sacrifices.

102 flying crews with 400 officers and men did not return. Fifty officers and men fell while willingly doing their duty, some on the ground, some in our defense against enemy air raids.

They gave all for Germany and our squadron and have the right to ask of us at this moment that we remain true and straight German men.

With a feeling of sorrow—but also with a feeling of pride, I take leave of my squadron today and thank you for the trust that you have had in me in times of crisis. If you now must endure hard work in a different Germany, then you, my men of NJG 4, can bear within you the feeling that you did all that was humanly possible to win this war for Germany.

Long live our beloved fatherland!
(signed) Schnaufer
Squadron Kommodore, NJG 4

On May 1, 1944, Schnaufer was promoted to Hauptmann. No one yet knew that he would begin an unequaled series of victories in German night fighting. As of March 1, 1944, he led IV./NJG as its commander.

The leadership of NJG 1, from left to right: Oberleutnant Weissflog (Intelligence Officer, staff of NJG 1), Schnaufer (Kommandeur, IV./NJG 1), Major Drewes (Kommandeur, III./NJG 1), Major Sutor, Leutnant Colonel Jabs (Kommodore, NJG 1), Hauptmann Dormann (Geschwaderstab), Major Förster (Kommandeur, I./NJG 1), Major von Bonin (Kommandeur, II./NJG 1), Hauptmann Knickmeier (Squadron Action Leader) and, lying, Hauptmann Greiner (Staff Hauptmann, 12./NJG 1).

His flight book recorded 2300 takeoffs, 1133 hours in flight, and 164 combat missions to date. Of his 121 kills, 114 were four-engine bombers. The awarding of the three highest German decorations for bravery between June and October 1944 indicates the overwhelming uniqueness of his success in German form. Thus, the most successful night fighter ended his career as a flight officer.

Nachtjagdgeschwader 4, with its Kommodore Heinz-Wolfgang Schnaufer, surrendered to the British. Finally they had the "Night Ghost", that legendary night fighter who had become a terror to their bomber crews. Along with other air officers, he was brought to Britain to be questioned.

He was something like a miracle man. One questioning was followed by another. Allied flight officers came and looked at Schnaufer. This young, good-looking man was the one who had shot 121 of their planes out of the skies! During the war, British propaganda had claimed that before his missions Schnaufer had been drugged with Lactal-B, for normally no man could hold out under such pressure. In British eyes it was abnormal that one man in one night could shoot down four or more bombers. Despite all the questioning and all of Schnaufer's denials, they could not and would not believe that his accomplishments were made without medicines or drugs.

But not only was Heinz-Wolfgang Schnaufer brought to Britain. The Messerschmitt 110 G-4/U 8 flown by him also made its last flight to Britain. The historic plane, with its 121 kill stripes on the rudder, was displayed in Hyde Park, London, and could be gawked at by the British for weeks. To this day the rudder is permanently on display at the Imperial War Museum in London in memory of the German night fighter who was the most effective and respected opponent of the Bomber command.

On July 1, 1944, Hans-Joachim Jabs (born 1917) succeeded Werner Streib as Kommodore of NJG 1. Jabs, originally trained as a combat pilot, was at first a fighter pilot, then a destroyer pilot, and began night fighting in November 1941. On October 1, 1940, he was honored with the Knight's Cross, and on March 3, 1944, with the 430th Oak Leaves. Jabs, an Oberstleutnant at the war's end, flew 510 missions, scored 28 night kills, and 19 victories with a destroyer and three in day combat.

Experts among themselves: Hauptmann Schnaufer, Hauptmann Breves, Hauptmann Augenstein (with head bandage), and Hauptmann Greiner.

On July 27, 1944, Wilhelm Gänsler received the Knight's Cross of the Iron Cross for taking part in shooting down 80 planes, 63 of them in Schnaufer's crew. With 115 participations, he was the most successful gunner in night fighting.

Schnaufer is probably checking the genuineness of the Knight's Cross awarded to Gänsler on July 27, 1944.

Hauptmann Martin Drewes congratulates Schnaufer on his 100th kill. At right is Helmut Lent.

August 2, 1944: Awarding of the Oak Leaves assigned on June 24, 1944, plus the swords won on July 30, 1944, by Heinz-Wolfgang Schnaufer and by Adolf Hitler at the Führer's "Wolf's Den" headquarters in East Prussia. Hitler, who had barely escaped the assassination attempted by Stauffenberg on July 20, 1944, could offer only his left hand because of an injury. From left: Friedrich Lang (SG 4), Erich Hartmann (JG 52), the most successful fighter pilot of all time, Schnaufer, Josef Fitz, ("Hermann Göring" Division), Eduard Skrizpek (KG 27), and Adolf Glunz.

Schnaufer's comrades give him a "good luck pig" for being awarded the swords. From left: Hauptmann Drewes, Leutnant Gräfe, Staff Doctor Schreiber, Schnaufer, and Major Rotter.

After catching diphtheria, Schnaufer was released from imprisonment in November 1945.

But when he returned from imprisonment to his homeland, Schnaufer did not rest on his laurels, but used his will power and energy to found a transport business with a North German friend on January 1, 1946, though he soon gave it up.

His creative powers seemed unbroken, as he then set out to build up his father's business, a wholesale liquor company and wine cellar, into a significant business. He founded his own branch offices. Former members of NJG 4, including his mechanic Wilhelm Gänsler and others who could not return to their homes in eastern Germany, were given jobs in the paternal business. Heinz-Wolfgang Schnaufer had only the goal of building up and expanding his father's firm, which he was able to do within two years. The small liquor factory became a large business with foreign contacts and partners, as well as its own sales facilities. And Heinz-Wolfgang Schnaufer was its leading spirit.

On July 13, 1950, Heinz-Wolfgang Schnaufer drove his Mercedes convertible along the road from Biarritz to Bordeaux. He was in France on business to supply and set up new business contacts. The speedometer indicated 80 kph. Out of a side road, its entrance concealed by a forest café, there suddenly came a truck at considerable speed that tried to cross the road without recognizing the right of way. All braking and steering maneuvers that Schnaufer tried could not prevent the accident. With a dull thud Schnaufer ran into the truck and his Mercedes caved in. At the same moment, the illegally loaded cargo of oxygen tanks tore loose from the bed of the truck, fell onto the road, and rolled into the ditch into which Heinz-Wolfgang Schnaufer had been thrown by the collision of his car, and in which he lay unconscious. The firefighters who were summoned rescued the badly injured man and an ambulance took him to a nearby clinic. There his identity was determined.

Fritz Rumpelhardt was decorated with the Knight's Cross on August 8, 1944, after taking part in 68 kills. He had flown with Schnaufer since July 1941 and was to become the most successful radioman of the night fighters with a total of 100 participations.

Oberstleutnant Lent, Heinz-Wolfgang Schnaufer, and Major Jabs, who together won 284 aerial victories.

Jabs and Schnaufer examine a P 47 Thunderbolt that was shot down by anti-aircraft guns on a low-flying raid.

Helmut Lent and Walter Kubisch. Kubisch, Lent's radioman since the war began, crashed with him in Paderborn on October 5, 1944, because of engine failure, and succumbed to his injuries the next day.

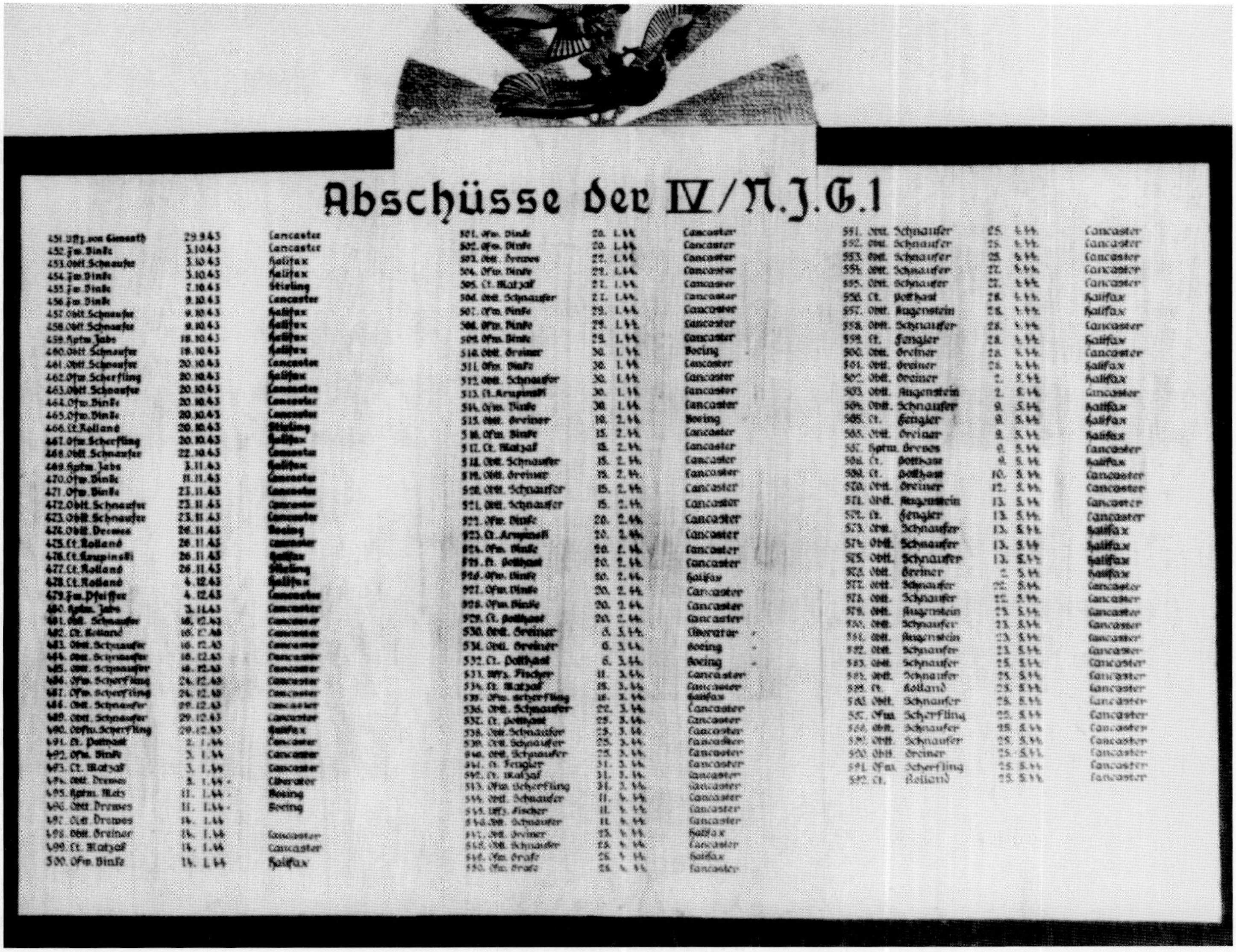

The list of IV./NJG 1's kills, on which Schnaufer's name appears 46 times.

Hauptmann Hermann Greiner (born 1920) succeeded Schnaufer on November 1, 1944, as Kommandeur of IV./NJG 1. Decorated with the Knight's Cross on July 27, 1944, and with the 840th Oak Leaves on April 17, 1945, Greiner took part in 204 combat missions and 51 aerial victories, including four on one day.

DIE BRILLANTEN FÜR SCHNAUFER

MAJOR WERNER HUSEMANN

HPTM. WERNER BAAKE

HPTM. HERBERT NÖLTER

OBERLT. WILHELM JOHNEN

On October 16, 1944, Schnaufer was awarded the 21st Diamonds to the Oak Leaves with Swords. He was the second night fighter, after Helmut Lent, to attain this high honor. The corps newspaper of the 1st Fighter Division, *Pauke Pauke*, reported on it in this special article.

The first official photo of the Schnaufer crew when he was awarded the Diamonds.

October 1944 in Dortmund: Schnaufer and his crew with some mechanics from a Dornier Do 215.

Kommodore of NJG 4 and his crew, Oberfeldwebel Gänsler and Leutnant Rumpelhardt, study theory.

Between night missions the young Kommodore Schnaufer also had to handle administrative duties, such as telephone calls, action reports, and talks with superior offices.

Two days later, on July 15, 1950, the most successful German night fighter died of the injuries he had suffered in the accident. After two more days his mother learned of the death of her son. His life had lasted only 28 years. He had mastered countless dangerous situations successfully. With death before his eyes daily in combat situations, he had risen from a young Leutnant to a mature major and squadron Kommodore in a very short time. Now his life had ended in a tragic manner.

In his home town of Calw the news of Heinz-Wolfgang Schnaufer's death spread like wildfire. Rumors circulated.

A murderous attack, belated revenge by the French Resistance, lured into a trap. . . .

Actually the rumors lasted for a time, while the French police sealed the coffin and turned it over to the next of kin only after long negotiations. But the suspicions turned out to be false. After the scene of the crash had been examined and the accident reconstructed, no evidence of an assassination or attack were found.

The population of the small Black Forest town of Calw accompanied the dead man to his last rest. The main street in a newly-built residential district was named in his honor.

On his tombstone can be read:

Here lies the best and never defeated night fighter
of World War II
Major and Squadron Kommodore
Heinz Wolfgang Schnaufer
1922-1950

Group picture with Kommodore: the most successful night-fighter crew, Rumpelhardt, Schnaufer, and Gänsler.

The mission order has arrived. The route of the approaching bomber packs is quickly studied on the map.

Schnaufer, as Major and Kommodore, never missed a chance to talk with the squadron's technicians.

In this photo one can see the flame-extinguisher tubes of the Bf 110. This apparatus served to make the exiting exhaust flames unseen by British bomber crews at night.

On this Bf 110 G-4, which Schnaufer and his crew and technicians are pushing into a hangar, the "slanted music," two MG 151 guns aimed diagonally upward, can be seen very well. With them the pilot could fly under the bombers and attack them with his upward-pointing weapons without coming under fire from their tail gunners.

Night fighter planes of the Bf 110 G-4 type. The antennas of the FuG 212 "Lichtenstein" night locating device can be seen on the planes. This system, developed by Telefunken and tested in the summer of 1941, was the first on-board searching radar of the German night fighters. It worked on a 60-cm wavelength at a range of 200 to 3000 meters. After increasing combat results it was established and was introduced to the troops as of 1942, although it affected the speed of the night fighters.

Schnaufer and his crew smile for a photographer.

A Bf 110 G-4 with the FuG 220 and SN-2 wide-angle location devices. They operated on a wavelength of 3.30 meters and were a further development of the FuG 212, which fell into British hands unharmed on May 9, 1943, and resulted in the deliberate throwing of "window" (metal foil strips) to cause orientation disturbances. On July 13, 1944, by a navigation error, an SN 2 also fell into British hands unharmed.

A Bf 110 G-4c with SN-2 radar and FuG 212, plus a 20 mm caliber MG 151 gun in the fuselage gondola.

From left: Gänsler, Schnaufer, and Rumpelhardt.

A Junkers Ju 88 G-2 with the antenna of the "Lichtenstein SN 2" night-fighting search device.

Bibliography:

Ries, Karl, & Ernst Obermaier, *Bilanz am Seitenleitwerk*, Verlag Dieter Hoffmann, 1970.

Obermaier, Ernst, *Die Ritterkreuzträger der Luftwaffe, Jagdflieger 1939-1945*, Verlag Dieter Hoffmann, 1989.

Lenfeld, Erwin & Franz Thomas, *Die Eichenlaubträger 1940-1945*, Weilburg Verlag, 1983.

Toliver, R. F., & T. J. Constable, *Das waren die deutschen Jagdfliegerasse, Stuttgart*, Motorbuch-Verlag, 1977.

Rumpephardt, Friedrich, *Meine Geschichte und die meiner Familie*, privately published, no date.

Held, Werner, & Holger Nauroth, *Die deutsche Nachtjagd*, Stuttgart, Motorbuch-Verlag, 1995.

Hinchcliffe, Peter, *Luftkrieg bei Nacht 1939-1945*, Stuttgart, Motorbuch-Verlag, 1998, Ralf Schumann Archives.

Private papers of retired Leutnant Friedrich Rumpelhardt, Mrs. Luise Schierholz

Federal Archives, Kornelimünster

Text & Research: Ralf Schumann

Photos: R. Schumann, F. Rumpelhardt, H. Growe, Mrs. Luise Schierholz, H. Diener, H.-J. Jabs, H. Greiner, J. Kammhuber, W. Streib, R. Fetzer, and J. Kraft

The most successful night-fighter team: Gänsler, Schnaufer, and Rumpelhardt stand before their plane. On 164 combat missions Schnaufer scored 121 night kills. His crew played a large part in them.

Schnaufer (second from right) with Streib (center), Augenstein, and Greiner at St.Trond.

The most successful German Night Fighters with 45 or more kills

Name	Rank	Squadron	Victories	Birth-Death	Orders
Schnaufer, Heinz-Wolfgang	Major	NJG 1, 4	121	1922-1950	RESB
Lent, Helmut	Oberst	NJG 1, 3	113	1918-1944	RESB
Prince zu Sayn-Wittgenstein, Heinrich	Major	NJG 2, 100	83	1916-1944	RES
Hergert, Wilhelm	Major	NJG 4	73	1910-1974	RE
Streib, Wolfgang	Oberst	NJG 1	68	1911-1986	RES
Meurer, Manfred	Hauptmann	NJG 1, 5	65	1919-1944	RE
Radusch, Günther	Oberst	NJG 1,2,3,5	65	1912-1988	RE
Schoenert, Rudolf	Major	NJG 1,5,10,100	65	1911-1985	RE
Roekker, Heinz	Hauptmann	NJG 2	64	1920-	RE
Welter, Kurt	Oberlt.	NJG 11	63	1916-1949	RE
Borchers, Walter	Oberstlt.	MJG 3, 5	59	1916-1945	R
Zorner, Paul	Major	MJG 3,5,100	59	1920-	RE
Becker, Martin	Hauptmann	NJG 6	58	1916-	RE
Rath, Gerhard	Hauptmann	NJG 2, 3	58	1920-1977	RE
Fransci, Gustav	Oberlt.	NJG 100	56	1914-1961	R
Kraft, Josef	Hauptmann	NJG 5, 6	56	1921-1994	RE
Strüning, Heinz	Hauptmann	NJG 1	56	1912-1944	RE
Frank, Hans-Dieter	Hauptmann	NJG 1	55	1919-1943	RE
Vikne, Heinz	Oberfeldw.	NJG 1	54	1920-1944	RE
Geiger, August	Hauptmann	NJG 1	53	1920-1943	RE
Hofmann, Werner	Major	NJG 5	52	1918-	R
Greiner, Hermann	Hauptmann	NJG 1	51	1920-	RE
Prinz zu Lippe-Weissenfeld, Egmont	Major	NJG 1, 3	51	1918-1944	RE
Jabs, Hans-Joachim	Oberstlt.	NJG 1	50	1917-	RE
Lütje, Herbert	Oberstlt.	NJG 1, 6	50	1918-1967	RE
Drewes, Martin	Major	NJG 1	49	1918-	RE
Kollak, Reinhard	Stabsfeldw.	NJG 1, 4	49	1915-1980	R
Hager, Johannes	Hauptmann	NJG 1	48	1920-1993	R
Drünkler, Ernst-Georg	Hauptmann	NJG 5, 3	47	1920-	R
Augenstein, Heinz	Hauptmann	NJG 1	46	1921-1944	R
Becker, Ludwig	Hauptmann	NJG 1	46	1911-1943	RE
Semrau, Paul	Hauptmann	NJG 2, 6	46	1915-1945	RE
Frank, Rudolf	Leutnant	NJG 3	45	1920-1944	RE
Lechner, Alois	Major	NJG 2, 5, 200	45	1911-1944	R

R = Knight's Cross; RE = R with Oak Leaves, RES = R with E and Swords, RESB = R with E, S, and Diamonds

The rudder of Major Schnaufer's Messerschmitt Bf 110 G-4 with the 121 night-fighter kill markings. It can still be seen at the Imperial War Museum in London.

This Bf 110 G-4b/Re of NJG 1 was taken by the British at the end of the war and, bearing British roundels and national markings, displayed at Farnborough in October and November 1945. Schnaufer's plane, on the other hand, was displayed in Hyde Park, London.

Rudolf Winnerl

An Oberfeldwebel of the Fighter Pilots with the Knight's Cross

Decorations:

4/29/1939	Luftwaffe Pilot's License: Land
4/30/1939	Airplane Pilot's Badge
5/1/1939	Service Medal 4th Class
6/25/1940	Iron Cross Second Class
3/31/1941	Blind Flying Certificate II (K)
7/5/1941	Front Flight Medal for Combat Pilots in Bronze
7/13/1941	Iron Cross First Class
10/4/1941	Front Flying Medal for Combat Pilots in Silver
2/23/1942	Honor Trophy for Special Achievement in Air War and Inclusion in the Luftwaffe Honors List
4/20/1942	Front Flight Medal for Combat Pilots in Gold
5/25/1942	German Cross in Gold
7/16/1942	Eastern Medal (Winter Combat in East 1941-42)
7/27/1942	Wound Medal in Black
10/13/1942	Front Flight Medal for Combat Pilots in Gold with Pendant
4/20/1943	Knight's Cross of the Iron Cross (presented on 4/27/1943)
12/31/1943	Demyansk Shield
12/1/1944	Wound Medal in Gold

Promotions:

5/2/1936	Gefreiter
10/1/1937	Obergefreiter
4/10/1939	Unteroffizier
10/1/1941	Feldwebel
8/1/1942	Oberfeldwebel

Combat Flights:

355 combat flights, 10 of them against France and 10 against Britain

Airplanes Flown:

Fw 44, He 72, Go 145, Ar 66, Ar 76, Fw 56, Ar 65, He 45, He 46, He 51, Fw 58, W 33, W 34, Ju 52, Do 17, Ju 86, He 111, and Ju 88, plus foreign Caudron, Saiman, and Vercelli L 3

Heinkel He 111 H-6, the Kommodore's plane of Oberst Angerstein (Marking V 4 + AA).

Rudolf Winnerl

Bomber pilots were seldom exposed to glory, as were, for example, fighter pilots, which were almost too much. It was not high kill scores or bold air battles that led them to win the Knight's Cross. A burden was more likely to be put on them in long-range flying, which often went to the limit in the loads they carried, with difficult navigation, fighting with the powers of navigation—without the enemy having a hand in it—and it demanded sacrifice before their actual tasks had begun. Through belts of searchlights by night and flying through anti-aircraft fire, concentrating only on the ordered target, they had just as hard a job to do as the fighters' duels in the sky demanded. They had to trust each other completely, and one was sacrificed to the other, but the combat pilots, whose crews consisted of three or more soldiers, were an effective team. The type of their action over long stretches, often without armed escorts, into the enemy's hinterlands, at night, in bad weather, over the sea, the attack formation in pack flying, the very quality of the slow bomber flight; all of that defined the face of a bomber flyer, who seemed quieter, with more stamina, and more settled externally than a fighter pilot. The bomber flyer always had to be on the lookout not to be cut off. Always keeping watch, always ready to jump in to help out or drop away. He must never lose sight of his actual task of delivering his bombs to the target.

Whether in horizontal flight or a dive, or on low-level raids on carpet-bombing, for the airman, as he was called in the jargon, there was only one thing: to fulfill the task and come safely back.

There were men with outstanding individual performances. Men with 300, 400 or more missions, who ranked among the aces of their service arm. The bomber packs of the German Luftwaffe, at the beginning of World War II, had a decisive role in the success of the German Wehrmacht. They never stood in the limelight of the public, and yet their accomplishments are not forgotten.

One of them was Oberfeldwebel Rudolf Winnerl, who received the high honor of the Knight's Cross of the Iron Cross for his flying and fighting success.

Ralf Schumann

Childhood and Family

Rudolf Winnerl, the son of miner Jacob Winnerl and his wife Anna, nee Schmalz, was born on March 15, 1916, in Lugau, Stolberg Borough, Chemnitz County, Kingdom of Saxony in the Erzgerbirge. After attending elementary school he learned the trade of a farmer. Entering the Hitler Youth in 1930, he was a leader in the Hitler Youth a year later. On June 5, 1935, he volunteered for the State Police in Chemniz, and was later transferred to the Army. There his military and infantry training took place. On May 2, 1936, he was promoted to Corporal.

Meanwhile a start had been made in the Luftwaffe, to a great degree in quickly increasing the flying units, at first with camouflage names, like "Traffic Inspection of the German Luft Hansa", and with makeshift warplanes. As of March 15, 1936, the formation of Kampfgeschwader 152 began; effective May 1, 1939, it officially was to be renamed Kampfgeschwader 1 "Hindenburg". Since personnel from the other armed forces were also heeded there, Winnerl, an Obergefreiter since October 1, 1937, volunteered for the Luftwaffe, as he was very interested and talented technically.

At the beginning of 1938 he was transferred to Pilot Training Regiment 21 in Magdeburg.

On April 10, 1949, Winnerl was promoted to Unteroffizier, and on June 25, 1940, he was awarded the Iron Cross II.

Summer 1936: Winnerl (X) marches as an Army Gefreiter. With blisters on his feet, he began to wish to travel by air.

After successful pilot training, Winnerl was trained as a fighter pilot in the 2nd Training Company at the big combat flying school of Tutow from October 2 to December 30, 1939, and after a short assignment at Aircraft Pilot School C in Zeltweg, he became a member of Kampfgeschwader 1 "Hindenburg" on January 2, 1940.

Combat Pilot Training and Front Service

On May 2, 1938, his pilot training began at Airplane pilot School 4 in Zeltweg. After that he was ordered to the Replacement Fighter Group 2 in Quedlinburg, and on April 10, 1939, he was promoted to Unteroffizier.

After successfully completing his aircraft pilot's training on single-engine planes, which Winnerl completed on April 29, 1939, he received a pilot's badge on 30 April and the 4th Class Service Medal on May 1, 1939. From October 2 to December 30, 1939, he was trained as a combat pilot at the Great Combat Pilot School in Tutow, where for the first time he flew multi-engine planes. Thus he was trained in planes like the Dornier Do 17, Junkers Ju 86, and Heinkel He 111, and introduced to the basis of combat flying. After being sent briefly to Air Pilot School C in Zeltweg, he became a member of the 9th Staffel of Kampfgeschwader 1 "Hindenburg" on January 2, 1940.

Here his front service began. On May 16, 1940, Winnerl took off from Ettinghausen at 3:15 P.M. in a Heinkel He 111 on his first combat mission. The target was the railroad station and troops in Berlagmont, France.

His second combat flight followed one day later. The target was the station at Perame. After being transferred back to the Cologne-Butzweilerhof airfield, he took off for his third mission, against troops in Armentieres, at 2:15 P.M. on 27 May.

After the British Expeditionary Forces that were located in France had withdrawn to Dunkirk, an attack on these troops in Dunkirk, Ostend, and Bruges took place on 28 May. This was Winnerl's fourth combat mission. He made two more flights with the 9th Staffel. On June 25, 1940, he was awarded the Iron Cross Second Class.

On July 6, 1940, he was transferred to the 7th Staffel. On the same day he took part in an attack on troops, but had to return to the airfield when his right engine failed.

On July 16, 1940, after he had flown another mission with the 7th Staffel on 10 June, he was finally moved to II. Gruppe of the 4th Staffel of the Geschwaders. The commander of the group was Major Benno Kosch (1900-1969).

The 4th Staffel of Kampfgeschwader 1 "Hindenburg", which was allowed to bear the traditional name since April 20, 1936, was the oldest fighter squadron in the Luftwaffe. Its origin went back to the Radio Navigation Institute at Tutow near Demmin, Pomerania. Established on April 1, 1934, this was the origin of combat flying.

From then on Wimmerl was to be in this Staffel as a fighter pilot. On December 22, 1940, he received his first home furlough.

He had already carried out ten missions against targets in France when he was sent to Blind Flight Training 2 at Neuburg on the Danube for blind flight training from January 13 to May 31, 1941. After returning to the squadron, Winnerl saw constant action with the 4th Staffel.

On July 17, 1940, Colonel Karl Angerstein, already a bomber pilot in World War I, took command of the "Hindenburg" Squadron as its Kommodore. On November 2, 1940, he was to receive the Knight's Cross for the outstanding achievements of the squadron and be promoted to Major General. He led the squadron until the Russian campaign began. In 1943 the squadron was again under his leadership when he took command of the 1st Flying Corps in Russia.

First combat missions against targets in France. Winnerl at the controls of his Heinkel He 111H-6.

Rudolf Winnerl (right) with members of his crew before a new mission during the French campaign.

"Eagle Day", the beginning of the air war on Britain (August 13, 1940), began at 9:00 A.M. Kampfgeschwader 1 "Hindenburg" took part in the first attacks on targets in Britain with the 1st Flying Corps of Senior General Ulrich Grauert (1899-1941) as part of Air Fleet 2, under the command of Generalfeldmarschall Albert

First long-range flight over the ocean in a Heinkel 111 E.

Kesselring (1885-1960). During the course of the air raids on Britain, Winnerl could record ten more combat missions, including attacks on the British fleet, large daylight raids on the mouth of the Thames, London, and ships in the Port of London.

On October 1, 1940, the success of the group, under the command of Benno Kosch, meanwhile promoted to Oberstleutnant, and always flying at the head of his group, could be suitably recognized with the awarding of the Knight's Cross.

In November 1940 II. Gruppe transferred to Münster-Handorf to be supplied with the Junkers Ju 88 plane.

On November 8, 1940, Oberleutnant Schlecht, nicknamed "Zack Zack", took command of the Staffel.

On March 10, 1941, the Staffel was moved back to France and to Rosieres field. As of January Hauptmann Otto Stams (1909-1976), formerly Staffelkapitän of the 7th Staffel, was in command of the group. Badly injured at the beginning of the Russian campaign,

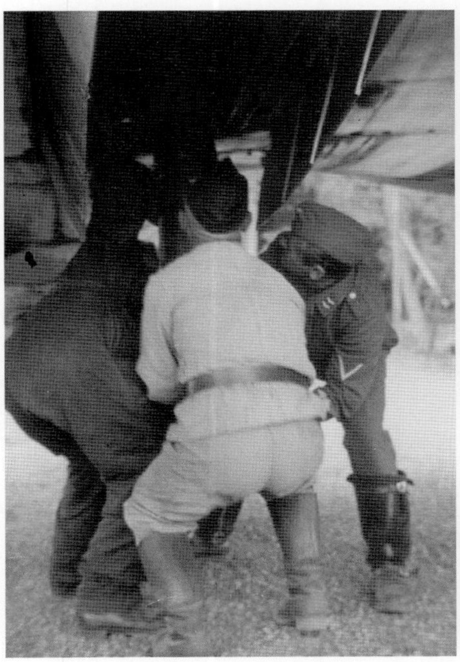

Preparations for a mission against targets in France. Winnerl's plane is loaded with explosive bombs.

Benno Kosch, Kommandeur of II./KG 1 "Hindenburg" during the western campaign and the Battle of Britain. Kosch was one of the first fighter pilots to receive the Knight's Cross on October 1, 1940. He was later Kommodore of KG 26 and KG 55.

he was honored for the success of his group by being awarded the Knight's Cross on August 1, 1942.

From now on came missions against Birmingham, Hull, Belfast, Portsmouth, and London again and again. In one of these raids on April 17, 1941, Oberfeldwebel Hermann's crew, with the Staffelkapitän Oberleutnant Schlecht flying as an observer, did not return.

On April 20, 1941, Knight's Cross bearer Oberleutnant Johannes Brandenburg (1910-1942) became Staffelkapitän of the 4th Staffel. Brandenburg, who had received the Knight's Cross on September 18, 1940, as Staffelkapitän of the 2./Dive Bomber Squadron "Immelmann", was highly esteemed by the crews and regarded as an outstanding pilot. Winnerl became his watchdog from then on.

In June 1941 II. Gruppe was withdrawn from British action and transferred to East Prussia, at Powunden, north of Königsberg. No one knew the reason for the transfer. On June 18, 1941, the flight personnel of the 4th Staffel arrived at Powunden. It had stayed longer in France to support the hard-fighting battleship "Bismarck" with attacks on the pursuing British warships. These attacks had to be given up after the "Bismarck" had ventured too far out into the Atlantic. There was just enough time to overhaul the planes. From Powunden the Staffel flew missions in the east after the Russian campaign began on June 22, 1941.

The "Black Gang" services a He 111 and changes its engine.

French campaign, 1940: Heinkel He 111 of the 9th Staffel flying against targets in France.

On French soil for the first time: destroyed French aircraft are examined.

Amiens was destroyed.

Winnerl's crew and their He 111 (V4 + AT) after taking the Amiens airfield.

Winnerl, who had meanwhile married Hildegard Kraekitz, the daughter of a tax secretary from Syke, near Bremen, had moved his residence there and felt very close to the native population.

The Junkers Ju 52 of the squadron staff. On the fuselage are the family arms of Generalfeldmarschalls von Hindenburg, after whom the squadron was named. Until 1940 they served as the squadron's coat of arms.

France has capitulated. Winnerl and members of the Hindenburg Squadron are seen on their way to Compienne.

A destroyed and abandoned French tank is examined on the road.

Beaten: French prisoners pass through the town.

In Compienne.

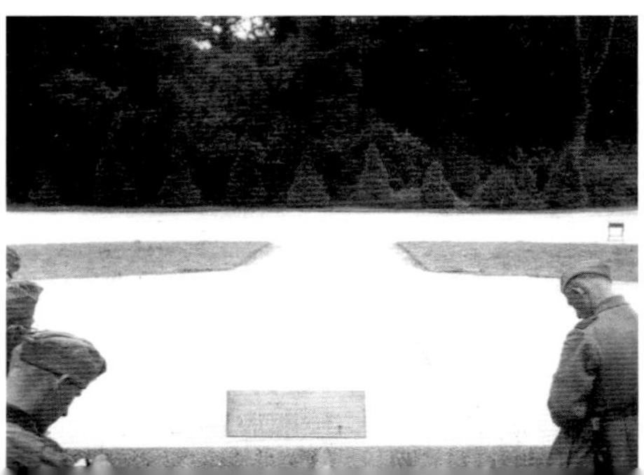

In December 1940, Oberleutnant Erich Schlecht took command of 4./KG 1 as Staffelkapitän and led it until April 1941.

In January 1941 Captain Otto Stams (1909-1976) took command of II./KG 1 "Hindenburg". Seriously wounded on June 27, 1941, Stams was decorated with the Knight's Cross on August 1, 1942, for the success of the group under his command.

On July 17, 1940, Oberst Karl Angerstein (1890-1985) took command of the "Hindenburg" Squadron as Kommodore. On November 2, 1940, he received the Knight's Cross for the outstanding achievements of the squadron.

The French campaign has ended, faces are happy, and Winnerl (sitting second from left) enjoys a smoke.

The rest period after the French missions is utilized. The Battle of Britain is yet to come.

Rest and recreation on the Baltic Sea. Winnerl (second from left) and his crew build up their strength before their missions against Great Britain.

The plane of the Staffelkapitän of 4./KG 1 takes off for Britain.

Firebombs are dropped over the target area.

This He 111 crashed short of its field because of heavy shot damage.

Well camouflaged, the planes wait for their next mission.

This He 111 of KG 1 crashed while flying over Cologne.

On April 20, 1941, Knight's Cross bearer Oberleutnant Johannes Brandenburg (born 1910) became Staffelkapitän of 4./KG 1 "Hindenburg". Brandenburg had already received the Knight's Cross on September 18, 1940, as Staffelkapitän of 2./Dive Bomber Squadron 2 "Immelmann". He fell south of Dobrow, Russia, on February 28, 1942.

A Heinkel He 111 of the 4th Staffel is loaded with a 500 kg bomb. At left in the picture is Artur Schumann, the author's father.

A crew returns from a night mission against Britain. The men's faces show the relaxed tension of the completed mission.

Russian Campaign and Knight's Cross

From the first day of the eastern campaign on, as of June 22, 1941, KG 1 "Hindenburg" was subordinate to the 1st Flying Corps in Gumbinnen, under the command of Generaleutnant Förster, subordinated in turn to Air Fleet 1 under Generaloberst Keller.

From then on the squadron was in the northern sector, making constant day and night missions against the air bases in Libau, Windau, Mittau, and Riga-Spilve, rail lines, troop movements and coastal fortifications, fighting the Soviet Baltic Sea Fleet, and against the Russian supply lines.

In action mainly in the northern sector, then in the central and southern sectors, Winnerl flew raids on Rshev, Moscow, and Stalingrad as the watchdog of Staffelkapitän and Knight's Cross bearer Johannes Brandenburg. In one mission against Stalingrad, Winnerl's plane was so badly damaged that he had to crash-land behind the Russian lines. In several night marches he and his crew fought their way back to their own lines.

June 1941, the calm before the storm. One day before "Operation Barbarossa", the beginning of the Russian campaign. Members of 4./KG 1 "Hindenburg" wait for the order to take action. At left with a newspaper is the Staffelkapitän, Oberleutnant Johannes Brandenburg.

In one of these raids, the Gruppenkommandeur, Captain Stams, was badly wounded on June 27, 1941, so that he was hospitalized and out of action for a long time.

Decorated on July 5, 1941, with the front flight medal in bronze for combat pilots and on July 13, 1941, with the Iron Cross First Class, Winnerl was promoted to Feldwebel effective October 1, 1941. Just three days later, on 4 October, he received the Front Flight Medal in silver.

On September 2, 1941, II. Gruppe was transferred to Insterburg, East Prussia, for retraining on the Junkers Ju 88 A-4, after having been in action against targets in Leningrad harbor and supply trains in the hinterlands after the closing of the ring around Leningrad. At this time Major Hans Keppler, who came from Kampfgeschwader 51 and had been Adjutant to Generaloberst Jeschonnek before his transfer to the Squadron, became Gruppenkommandeur. On August 20, 1942, while he was Geschwaderkommodore, he was awarded the Knight's Cross for the success of the group. A few days later, on September 3, 1942, he fell at Mag, Russia.

At the beginning of October the group was in front action again. Also in October the weather necessitated a transfer of III. Gruppe to Dno and II. Gruppe to Staraja-Russa. Now the costly winter war began, in which the focal points of the action consisted of fighting supply lines across the frozen Lake Ladoga and army support. In December II. Gruppe was also moved to Dno.

The year 1942 began with large-scale Soviet attacks east of Lake Ilmen. Ceaseless missions were required to support the Army. Now Winnerl was constantly in front service over Russia and flew on all the Staffel's missions. His front-flight numbers grew quickly, and he now ranked among the most experienced pilots in the group. On February 23, 1942, he was awarded the Trophy of Honor for special achievement in the air war by the Supreme Commander of the Luftwaffe and accepted in the Luftwaffe Honors List.

On February 27, 1942, the 4th Staffel of Kampfgeschwader 1 "Hindenburg" could record their 1000th combat mission.

Junkers Ju 88s of 4./KG 1 "Hindenburg" fly toward Russian targets on June 23, 1941.

A new mission is before them. Rudolf Winnerl (second from left) and his crew stand before their Ju 88 A-4.

One day later a serious blow struck them. On 28 February the Staffel took off to attack troops in the Kastenwald, southeast of Dobrovo, ten kilometers southwest of Cholm. Winnerl flew that day, as always before, as Staffelkapitän Oberleutnant Brandenburg's watchdog. After a successful attack, a crew reported by radio that they still had bombs on board. Brandenburg ordered a new attack and accompanied that plane. At this time the attack of Ju 87 dive bombers was already underway, just five minutes away to the side of the Staffel's attack. Brandenburg's Ju 88 was hit by a bomb from a dive-bomber and his plane was torn to pieces. Oberleutnant Brandenburg and his crew were killed. Winnerl, who had to see the fate of his captain, could not prevent the attack of the dive bombers because of their different radio frequencies. All warnings that he cried out to his leader met without success. Later, advancing army troops found the wreckage of the plane and could identify Brandenburg by his Knight's Cross. This loss was a severe blow for the Staffel and the squadron.

On March 1, 1942, Oberleutnant Wachholz took command of the Staffel. Winnerl remained in action, and his front flights increased. During the month of March the Staffel's attacks to support the Army continued. Flights often had to be made in bad weather, since the Army urgently needed support. On 20 March the attack to relieve the troops encircled by the Russians at Demyansk and Cholm began.

On March 29, 1942, Winnerl already had made his 200th combat flight against targets in Russia. On 20 April he received the Front Flight Medal in Gold.

Among his crew were his radioman Christian Heil, his mechanic Johann Gürtler, and his observer Kurt Seidel, always his loyal companions. Heil and Gürtler later received the German Cross in Gold.

On April 24, 1942, the former Technical Officer of II. Gruppe, First Leutnant Klaus Mohr, took command of the Staffel, after Oberleutnant Wachholz had been sent to the Flight School at Graz. Mohr was to command it until June 1943.

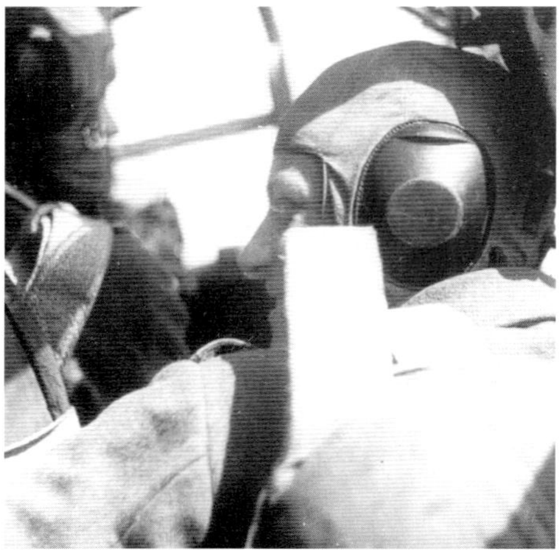

A m ssion over Russia—all nerves are tense.

Air view of damaged Novgorod.

Riga Spilve, where the extent of the German air raids can be seen.

The wreckage at the Riga-Spilve airport.

A shot-down Russian Li-2 transport plane.

An idyllic scene at an airfield in the east.

At Easter 1942 Winnerl took part in a large-scale daylight attack on ships in the harbor of Leningrad, where he was able to damage a 5000-ton troop transport. On further missions he was able to sink three other ships on June 25 and July 5 and 6, 1942. On July 25, 1942, he was able, despite severe shot damage to his Junkers Ju 88 and a head wound, to fly safely back to his takeoff point.

On June 27, 1942, he received the Wound Medal in Black. The awarding of the German Cross in Gold, already conferred on May 25, 1942, and his promotion to Oberfeldwebel on August 1, 1942, were the rewards for his heroic actions. Meanwhile he and his crew had succeeded in sinking a Soviet submarine during their attacks on ships in the Gulf of Finland.

Summer 1941 in Russia: the men of 4./KG 1 "Hindenburg" live in tents.

On August 20, 1941, Winnerl, at left with his comrades, was honored with the Iron Cross I, and on October 1, 1941, he was promoted to Feldwebel.

Autumn 1941: Rudolf Winnerl's Ju 88 is refueled. The steady rain that not only made missions difficult also softened the ground so much that taking off with the heavy fully fueled and munitioned plane was sometimes impossible.

October 28, 1941, 8:30 A.M.: A photo of a target for Sergeant Winnerl's crew, a railroad break 20 km east of Point 792.

In July 1942, Major Herbert Lorch (1913-1942) had taken command of II. Gruppe. Lorch, who had been familiar with the command of the group from March 2 to June 30, 1942, did not return from a combat mission against targets near Bryansk. He has been listed as missing since then. He was posthumously awarded the Knight's Cross.

Then came further raids from the Bryansk field into the Kaluga, Rshev, and Orel areas, where enemy breakthrough attempts were shattered.

On 10 September the Staffel was transferred to Siverskaya field in the Leningrad area. At the end of December 1942 II. Gruppe was sent to Königsberg-Neuharsen for refreshment.

On October 23, 1942, Rudolf Winnerl received the Front Flight Medal in gold with pendant for his combat missions to date. Because of his already attained success and his experience as a pilot, in which he had brought his plane safely back to the field on one engine, he was appointed lead pilot.

A Ju 88 of 4./KG 1 "Hindenburg" is loaded with a 500 kg bomb for the next mission.

Winter 1941: Winnerl in the cockpit of his Ju 88 A-4. The plane has been given temporary winter paint.

Brandenburg and Winnerl discuss the next mission.

Last instructions to the crew.

The Staffelkapitän, Oberleutnant Brandenburg (second from right), is reported to by the other crews after their return from a mission. Rudolf Winnerl, second from left, flew as Brandenburg's wingman at that time.

Christmas in the east, 1941.

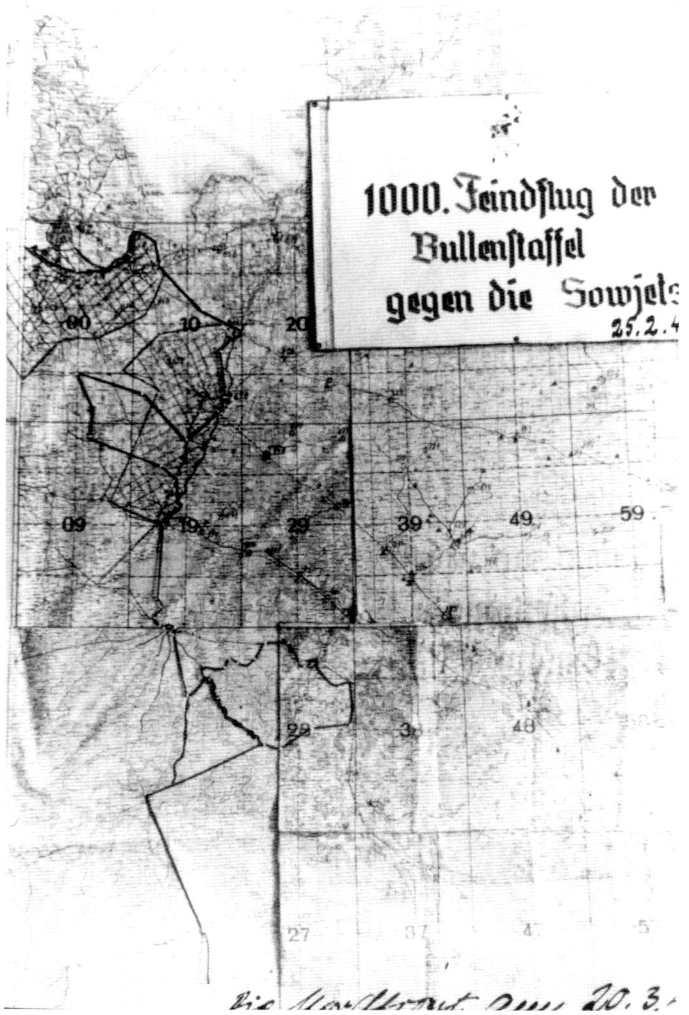

On February 25, 1942, 4./KG 1 "Hindenburg" flew their 1000th combat mission.

In April 1942 First Lieutenant Klaus Mohr took command of 4./KG 1. As Hauptmann and Kommandeur of II./KG 1, Mohr was lost in 1943 during a combat flight over the Mediterranean Sea.

Oberfeldwebel Alfred Behrendt, Chief of 4./KG 1 "Hindenburg".

At the end of October 1943 he had to make an emergency landing behind enemy lines because of enemy shot damage during a combat mission against Leningrad. He and his crew remained unharmed and undiscovered by Russian troops. Utilizing the darkness, the crew fought its way through to its own lines after several days of traveling on foot and reached their takeoff point. Their comrades were delighted to see them again. This new "birthday" was followed by a four-week recovery furlough in Kitzbühl. Then it was back to the front for one mission after another.

On March 19, 1943, Oberstleutnant Horst von Riesen took over as the new Kommodore of the squadron after the former commander, Heinrich Lau (1911-1956), who was awarded the Knight's Cross in that position on May 10, 1943, had been transferred to the staff of the Attack Leader England (General Peltz).

On April 20, 1943, Winnerl's fighting and flying success were recognized by the awarding of the Knight's Cross. By that time he had made some 300 combat flights and sunk one

The flag of 4./KG 1 "Hindenburg", the "Bull Staffel".

At Lake Pelpus.

The field air base by Lake Pelpus. A Ju 88 is being serviced.

A Junkers Ju 88 of 4./KG 1 "Hindenburg" comes in to land on the airfield by Lake Pelpus.

Camp life by Lake Pelpus for Winnerl and his crew.

U-boat and two observation craft, destroyed four anti-aircraft and artillery positions, ten tanks, nine bunkers, three ammunition and one supply depot, eleven transport trains and damaged a 5000-ton troop transport, temporarily cut 19 rail lines, and supported the Army's hard fighting by attacking enemy troop assemblies and supply lines, as well as supply trips into the pocket at Demyansk and Cholm.

Thus Rudolf Winnerl became the second Knight's Cross bearer of the 4th Staffel, and one of seven members of II. Gruppe of the "Hindenburg" Squadron to receive this high honor.

On December 31, 1943, he was also decorated with the Demyansk Shield for his combat flights into the Demyansk pocket, in which he had flown supplying, relief, and disturbing missions.

February 1942, south of Leningrad: A crew is greeted with honors after their 200th combat flight.

March 29, 1943: Rudolf Winnerl's 200th combat mission is celebrated. The comrades and Oberleutnant Wachholz congratulate them appropriately.

March 15, 1942: Winnerl was able to bring his crew and plane home and land safely on one engine after heavy shot damage.

On their "birthday" the crew is congratulated by Oberleutnant Wachholz and their comrades.

A Ju 88 A-4 of the 8th Staffel.

A burden that brings death.

Easter 1942: A target photo for Winnerl's crew. A Russian 5000-ton troop transport which they sank in Leningrad harbor.

In May 1942 Generaloberst Alfred Keller visits the group at Pleskau. Here he talks with members of the 4th Staffel.

On May 25, 1942, Winnerl was decorated with the German Cross in Gold. The Group Commander, Major Lorch, presents the medal to him.

Best wishes on his attainment also come from Oberleutnant Klaus Mohr.

Winnerl (second from right) with his crew, gunner Unteroffizier Gürtler (right), Unteroffizier Seidel (second from left), and radioman Unteroffizier Heil (left) after Gürtler (on June 5, 1942) and Heil (on May 27, 1942) had also received the German Cross in Gold.

Winnerl before taking off for the Gulf of Finland with the task of attacking ships.

The Staffel painter keeps score on Winnerl's plane. Four A-A batteries and three ships are the score to date on the rudder.

On July 25, 1942, Winnerl, despite his head wound and severe shot damage, was able to land his plane at his home field in Dno. On the occasion of an honor by the group's Kommandeur, Major Lorch, and the conferring of the Wound Medal on Winnerl, as well as awards to other worthy crews, the group turned out before their quarters. To the left of the traffic sign is Rudolf Winnerl with one eye bandaged.

In July 1942 Major Herbert Lorch (1913-1942) took command of II. Gruppe. Lorch, who led the squadron from March 2 to June 30, 1942, did not return from a combat mission near Bryansk on August 19, 1942, and has been listed since then as missing. He was posthumously awarded the Knight's Cross on January 5, 1943.

Major Lorch congratulates Winnerl on his flying achievements and awards him the Wound Medal in Black, which was assigned to him on July 27, 1942. He was also promoted to Oberfeldwebel effective July 25, 1942.

This occasion was also celebrated. The Staffelkapitän, Oberleutnant Mohr, takes the occasion to congratulate Winnerl personally.

Winnerl after his 300th combat flight.

Winnerl with his crew.

On this occasion, a good drink from the bottle.

On September 30, 1942, Oberfeldwebel Adolf Kraus (born 1916) crashed fatally in bad weather on takeoff for his 351st combat flight. His whole crew was lost with him. Kraus, one of the most experienced pilots of the squadron, had belonged to the 4th Staffel since May 1941 and was posthumously awarded the Knight's Cross.

After the death of Major Lorch, Major Hans Keppler (born 1912) succeeded him. He too would be rewarded for the success of the group with the Knight's Cross on August 20, 1942. A few days later, on September 3, 1942, Keppler fell near Mag, Russia.

Winter 1942-43: The lodging of 4./KG 1. At left in the picture is the author's father.

Schaulen, Russia, January 1943, Lake Ladoga, Russia: Winnerl takes off on another combat mission . . .

. . . and later returns successfully.

The Staffel's 2000th combat flight is also observed suitably.

Oberfeldwebel and Knight's Cross bearer "Rudi" Winnerl.

The N.C.O. Corps of 4./KG 1, led by Spiess Oberfeldwebel Alfred Behrendt, on the way to the ceremony. Second from left is Artur Schumann, the author's father.

A sip from the Cup of Honor after its awarding by the Staffelkapitän, Oberleutnant Klaus Mohr.

After the award ceremony, Rudolf Winnerl marches with Oberleutnant Mohr between the comrades in attendance.

His comrades honor their new "hero" appropriately.

The group turns out for the conferring of the Knight's Cross on Oberfeldwebel Winnerl.

The band greets the new Knight's Cross bearer at the railroad station.

The Knight's Cross is awarded on April 18, 1943.

Knight's Cross bearer Rudolf Winnerl among his comrades.

In the ranks of his comrades, wearing the Knight's Cross.

Knight's Cross bearer Oberleutnant Otto Edler von Ballasko (born 1919), Staffelkapitän of 9./KG 1, congratulates Rudolf Winnerl for his high honor.

On the evening when the Knight's Cross was awarded a banquet took place. Winnerl (left), an Army general (unknown), and Oberleutnant Mohr dine among their comrades.

From left: Heil, Winnerl, and Gürtler.

Captain Peter-Heinz Nolte served as Captain of 4./KG 1 after Oberleutnant Mohr.

A crew of the "Bull Staffel" after returning from their 300th combat flight. The members congratulate them appropriately.

In the east, 1943: A crew of 4./KG 1, from left to right: the pilot, Unteroffizier Kurzweil; radioman Corporal Oldag; observer Unteroffizier Steiner; and mechanic Gefreiter Rückes.

Farewell from Hauptmann Nolte on the planned transfer to Italy. Here he says farewell to Hauptmann Behrendt . . .

Italian Theater of War, Wounding and War's End

On September 11, 1943, I. and II. Gruppe were transferred to Italy. There they were supposed to see action against the Allied landing troops on Sicily. Then came joint actions from the Viterbo takeoff base against the landing fleet and the supply traffic, which caused heavy losses. Since the superior forces were too numerous, the squadron moved again to their new base, Foggia.

Now came difficult and costly actions against supply shipping and support points in North Africa from Bizerte and Algiers, as well as on Siracusa, Palermo, and Augusta in Sicily and Allied air bases. After Italy had capitulated on September 8, 1943, the squadron moved to Airasca after turning the remaining planes over to Kampfgeschwaders 54 and 76, and at first took on defensive tasks for two months, plus the protection of military facilities in the area of the former 1. Squadra Aera in the Turin-Milan area. Winnerl, who had been on furlough since 11 September, returned directly to Italy.

On November 13, 1943, Oberfeldwebel Winnerl, as the officer on duty, was making a nightly guard check on the edge of an airfield in Italy when he was lured into a trap and shot in the head, which left him almost completely crippled, so badly so that he was no longer capable of service. For him the non-flying task had become his fate, for he had not been able to fly a single mission there.

Until that fateful day Rudolf Winnerl had flown the following types of airplanes during his training and service: Fw 44, He 72, Go 145, Ar 66, Ar 76, Fw 56, Ar 65, He 45, He 46, He 51, Fw 58, W 33, W 34, Ju 52, Do 17, Ju 86, He 111, and Ju 88, plus the foreign Caudron, Saiman, and Vercelli L 3 models.

He had also flown 355 missions against targets in France, Great Britain, and Russia successfully.

. . . and here to Rudi Winnerl.

Bibliography:
Ralf Schumann Archives (all rights reserved by author)
Estate of Rudolf Winnerl, privately owned
Ralf Schumann, *Die Ritterkreuzträger des Kampfgeschwader 1 "Hindenburg" 1933-1945*, Zweibrücken, Verlag VDM-Nickel, 2000

Photos:
Ralf Schumann Archives (all rights reserved by author)
Estate of Rudolf Winnerl

Acknowledgments:
The author's thanks go particularly to Frau Hildegard Winnerl, who made it possible, through her permission and search of the estate of her late husband, for this book to be written. Likewise Herr Franzke of UNITEC Medienvertrieb, who made it possible to reach a broad spectrum of readers by publishing this documentation in his publishing house. Also to my wife and two sons, who did without me in my free time so this book could come into being.

Artur Schumann (born 1920), the author's father, flew as a mechanic in 4./KG 1 against targets in Britain, Russia, and Sicily. As a sergeant he came in the autumn of 1944 to the Berlin Bear Division after the squadron was disbanded, and took part in the fighting in the west as a platoon leader in Grenadier Regiment 477, fighting against the Allied invasion troops in the Ardennes offensive.

Before the transfer to Italy, a few days of rest on the Moselle.

The Knight's Cross Bearers of Kampfgeschwader 1 "Hindenburg"
Who while they belonged to the squadron received the Knight's Cross of the Iron Cross and its higher levels.

Name	Awarded	At Rank	Last Rank	Birth/Death
Angerstein, Karl	11/2/1940	Oberst. & Comd. KG 1	Generalleut.	12/4/1890-9/20/1985
Ballasko, Otto Edler von	8/13/1942	Oberlt. Capt 9./KG 1	Hauptmann	9/29/1919
Brueckner, Wolfgang	12/5/1943	Oberlt Capt. 3./KG 1	Hauptmann	5/26/1920-7/14/1943
Hart, Rolf	10/15/1942	Leut, Pilot 9./KG 1	Oberleutnant	4/13/1921-3/9/1943
Keppler, Hans	8/20/1942	Major, Cmdr III./KG 1	Oberstleut.	2/11/1912-9/3/1943
Kosch, Benno	10/1/1940	Oberstlt Cmdr II./KG 1	Oberst	3/12/1900-1969
Kraus, Adolf	11/25/1942	Oberfdw., Pilot 4./KG 1	Oberfeldw.	12/26/1916-9/30/1942
Lau, Heinrich	5/10/1943	Major, Comd. KG 1	Oberstleutnant	9/15/1911-9/14/1956
Lindinger, Eduard	12/9/1942	Feldw. Pilot 7./KG 1	Oberfeldwebel	1/17/1915
Lorch, Herbert	1/5/1943	Major,Comm.II./KG 1	Major	4/13/1913-8/19/1942
Maier, Kurt	11/16/1942	Oberlt. Capt.3/KG 4		1/21/1911-
674th Oak Leaves	12/6/1944	Captain 9./KG 1	Hauptmann	2/11/1952
Mevissen, Kurt	9/19/1942	Feldw. Pilot 9./KG 1	Oberleutnant	3/29/1917-10/29/1952
Michael, Hermann	10/9/1943	Hauptmann, Staff	Hauptmann	11/13/1916-7/5/1943
Captain 8./KG 1				
Sprung, Helmut	11/12/1943	Leut., Pilot 7./KG 1	Oberleutnant	11/27/1921-10/14/1955
Stams, Otto	8/1/1942	Hauptm., Comm.II./KG 1	Oberstlt.	4/5/1909-5/17/1976
Sumpf, Hans	8/20/1942	Oberlt, Capt 5./KG 1	Hauptmann	3/27/1915-3/26/1942
Taeger, Erich	10/2/1942	Oberlt, Capt 7./KG 1	Hauptmann	8/5/1919
Trenke, Johann	9/5/1944	FJ-Feldw., Pilot 6./KG 1	Resv. Leut.	8/3/1919-4/29/1957
Tscherning, Willy	11/18/1944	Oberfdw, Rdmn 9./KG 1 Oberfeldw.	6/15/1917-	
Wilhelm, Hans-Joachim	10/29/1944	Oberlt, Pilot 9./KG 1	Oberleutnant	5/25/1922-4/13/1945
Winnerl, Rudolf	4/18/1943	Oberfdw., Pilot 4./KG 1	Oberfeldbl.	3/15/1916-2/26/1991

[Note: Comm. = Kommandeur; Comd. = Kommodore, FJ = Fahnenjunker, Rdmn = Radioman; Oberleutnant = 1st Lieutenant, Oberstleutnant = Oberstleutnant]

Reserve Hospital and War's End

On November 27, 1943, he was taken to the Luftwaffe Officers' Hospital 39779 and was transferred to the Reserve Hospital in Nörtlingen on July 8, 1944. After further treatment, he was transferred again to Reserve Hospital IV Bertholdschule in Würzburg. Sent to Reserve Hospital V in Bamberg on September 23, 1944, he was awarded the Wound Medal in gold on December 1, 1944, because of his severe wound. Then on February 13, 1945, his wife Hildegard picked him up there and took him by train to Syke. Accompanied by her mother and an assigned medic, they traveled from Bamberg via Schweinfurt, Würzburg, and Hannover to Bremen, surviving several Allied bomb attacks on the cities and depots they passed through. After five days they reached Syke, where they experienced the arrival of the Canadian and later British troops. Because of his condition and the resulting care that he needed he was spared imprisonment.

Successful on 355 missions, the war ended for him in his home town in the care of his wife Hildegard. Their marriage produced two daughters.

Rudolf Winnerl, despite his physical disability, never lost contact with his comrades. He died on February 26, 1991, in Syke, Diepholz County, Hannover Government District, State of Niedersachsen, and found his last resting place there.

The Tradition Organization "Kampfgeschwader Hindenburg" placed a wreath on his grave in memory of their former squadron comrade, pilot, and bearer of the Knight's Cross.

September 11, 1943, in Speyer before the transfer flight to Italy. Winnerl (center) and members of the unit wait for loading. This was to be his last flight.

Some Planes Flown by Rudolf Winnerl during his Training

Focke Wulf Fw 44 "Stieglitz"

Heinkel He 46

Heinkel He 72 "Kadett"

Arado Ar 66

Focke Wulf Fw 58 "Weihe"

Heinkel He 72

Junkers W 34 Hi

Dornier Do 17

Caudron C 445 "Goeland"

Above: A Ju 88 A-4 of the 8th Staffel. Below: The Winnerl crew in Kaunas (Kovno) on April 24, 1943 from left: Radioman Feldwebel Christian Heil, Pilot Oberfeldwebel Winnerl, Mechanic Unteroffizier Johann Gürtler, and Observer NCO Nagel.

Hermann Graf

The First Fighter Pilot with 200 Air Victories

Decorations:

12/15/1941	Cup of Honor for Special Achievement in Air War
1/24/1942	Knight's Cross of the Iron Cross
4/0/1942	German Cross in Gold
5/17/1942	93rd Oak Leaves to the Knight's Cross of the Iron Cross
5/19/1942	11th Swords to the Oak Leaves of the Knight's Cross
6/19/1942	5th Diamonds to the Oak Leaves of the Knight's Cross

Promotions:

5/1/1940	Leutnant der Reserve (effective)
5/19/1942	Oberleutnant der Reserve
6/0/1942	Hauptmann der Reserve
10/1/1942	Major
5/1/1944	Oberstleutnant
0/0/1945	Oberst

Combat Flights:

830 on the eastern and western fronts

Kills:

212 confirmed and 40 unconfirmed aerial victories
(including 10 in the west, 6 four-engine bombers and 1 Mosquito)

Commodore Positions:

Commander of Fighter Group 50	3/43-10/43
Commodore of JG 1 "Oesau"	10/43-11/10/43
Commodore of JG 11	11/16/43-3/29/44
Commodore of JG 52	10/1/44-5/8/45

The pictures in this book come mainly from war literature of the time; their poor quality is due to the poor-quality paper of the last war years. Despite the most modern computer reworking, it was not always possible to attain good quality. Despite this we have decided to publish them, so as to emphasize the historical associations with the personality of Hermann Graf.

With his 81 aerial victories, Baron Manfred von Richthofen ranked highest among the fighter pilots of all participating nations at the end of World War I. He was the model for all German fighter pilots in World War II. When the war began in 1939, it was never imagined that his success would be repeated, much less exceeded with higher totals.

When Werner Mölders became the first fighter pilot to achieve 100 aerial victories, this was a splendid achievement for most fighter pilots. But as the war's actions expanded into various theaters of war, the German Luftwaffe had to face new and greater opponents.

So it was finally Hermann Graf who became the first fighter pilot to attain the unimaginable total of 200 aerial victories, and in only thirteen months. He himself had never thought that he would be the one to write aerial history and rank among the ten best fighter pilots.

Still a Reserve Unteroffizier when the war began, he was to rise from a simple pilot to an Oberst and a squadron Kommodore—a picture-book career. Despite all the honors and the awarding of the highest medals for bravery, he preferred the daily battle to staff activity. Thus he was the only bearer of the Diamonds in daylight missions who flew as a unit leader in the defense of the Reich and, despite a ban on flying, could score a string of kills.

Along with a handful of other experts in their service arm, he formed a cadre of successful fighter aces who understood their craft in JG 52, the squadron of the German Luftwaffe with 10,800 confirmed aerial victories and thus the most kills in World War II. Names like Alfred Grislawski (1919-2003), Walter Süss (1912-1943), Leopold Steinbatz (1918-1942), and Heinrich Füllgrabe (1916-1945) are closely linked with Hermann Graf's success. Together they scored 579 confirmed aerial victories.

The 9th Staffel of Jagdgeschwader 52, the "Karaya Squad" or "Red Hunters", in which these men flew, was respected and feared by their Soviet opponents. Hermann Graf, rising from Unteroffizier to Jagdfliegeroffizier, ranks ninth in the list of the best fighter pilots of all wars and nations, and thus ranks among the aces of this service.

Ralf Schumann

Training and First Action as a Fighter Pilot

Engen, the birthplace of Hermann Graf.

Hermann Graf was born in Hegau, Baden on October 24, 1912, as the youngest son of a smith. What with the poor conditions in which he grew up, he could not attend a high school. This meant that later, when he joined the Wehrmacht, he could not become a career officer. From 1933 on he was interested in glider flying, and as of 1936 he turned to powered flight. After he finished his schooling he was an apprentice smith, later worked in a factory, and then took additional administrative training with the Engen city government, finishing it as an administrative assistant. After he had passed all glider tests and made a name for himself as a soccer player he joined the Wehrmacht in 1936.

When he finished his military service, he joined the Reserve with the goal of attending the Flying School at Karlsruhe. Afterward, as a Gefreiter in the Reserve, he returned to the social service department of the city of Engen and continued his work as an administrative assistant. After further Reserve service, in which he gained a Stunt Pilot's License 1, Civilian Flight License and B-2 Certificate, he was a fully qualified pilot in the German Luftwaffe in the spring of 1938. In April 1939 he saw more Reserve service, took Unteroffizier training, and became a Reserve officer's aide.

Deciding to be a fighter pilot, Graf volunteered for the Luftwaffe on July 15, 1939. With a lot of luck, for at that time there was an order not to admit any more Reserves into the active fighter units, Hermann Graf was assigned to the Abling Fighters on July 31, 1939. He joined I.Gruppe of JG 51, where he was promoted to Feldwebel of the Reserve and assigned to the 2nd Staffel. After World War II began on September 1, 1939, Graf flew 21 front missions on the western border without firing a single shot. On January 18, 1940, he was transferred to the Merseburg Replacement Group as a fighter-pilot trainer.

In July 1940 Graf, promoted to Leutnant on May 1, 1940, went to the 9th Staffel of JG 52. He owed this move to the new Group Kommandeur, who commanded the 2nd Staffel of JG 51. This was Major Gotthard Handrick, Olympian Pentathlon athlete in 1936, who was impressed by the 28-year-old Reserve's soccer skills and allowed him to move to a front unit. With two pilots from among his students, Graf now went to Berlin. These two pilots were to accompany him on his future career as a fighter pilot. They were Alfred Grislawski and Leopold Steinbatz.

But the unit's planned transfer to the Channel coast of France was canceled, and Graf moved to Romania with JG 52. There he served as an instructor with the military mission, and then took part in Operation "Merkur", the action on the Greek Mediterranean island of Crete. By this time Graf had entered some 50 front missions in his flight book without firing a single shot at an enemy plane. In July 1941, when Graf came to the eastern front as a Feldwebel in the 9th Staffel of JG 52, his remarkable career began.

His long-awaited first aerial victory came on August 3, 1941, during the recently begun Russian campaign. After this step success came rapidly. In the ensuing months Graf learned how to beat the Russian pilots with their own weapons. Graf specialized

Flight Student Hermann Graf, in winter attire, stands before a Focke Wulf Fw 44 "Stieglitz".

Hermann Graf in summer attire by the propeller of a Focke Wulf Fw 44 "Stieglitz".

Hermann Graf with his mechanics and helpers.

in defeating the Russian pilots where they liked best to fight, at low altitudes. That won him the nickname "King of the Hedge-Hoppers". His rapidly increasing string of victories won Graf a promotion to Leutnant of the Reserve in December, plus the Cup of Honor for special achievement in aerial war on December 15, 1941, because of his bravery before the enemy.

Along with his friend and wingman "Bazi" Steinbatz, he gained great success in the next weeks against Russian fighters and bombers. Within the next nine months he was to win the four highest awards of the German Wehrmacht and become the nightmare of the Soviet pilots. On January 24, 1942, Graf gained the Knight's Cross of the Iron Cross for his 45 aerial victories. Feldwebel Steinbatz followed his example and was likewise awarded the Knight's Cross on February 24, 1942, after 42 kills. In the spring Hermann Graf's meteoric rise finally began; it was to make him the most spectacular member of the Luftwaffe.

Munich-Neubiberg Airfielc: After finishing flight training, pilot Hermann Graf stands beside a Focke Wulf Fw 54 "Weihe'.

On August 4, 1941, Graf shot down a Polikarpov I-16 a kilometer southeast of Kiev, his first aerial victory.

In July 1940, after briefly belonging to JG 51, Graf was transferred to JG 52. This is the squadron's emblem.

Alfred Grislawski (1919-2003), seen here as an Unteroffizier, was transferred to JG 52 with Graf. He was also to become one of the best German fighter pilots.

Major Hubertus von Bonin (1911-1943) led III. Gruppe of JG 52, to which Graf had been transferred, from October 1, 1941, to July 5, 1943. On December 21, 1942, he received the Knight's Cross. He fell near Gorodok, in the Soviet Union, on December 15, 1943.

Planes of JG 52 on an airfield in Russia.

On December 15, 1941, Hermann Graf was awarded the Cup of Honor for special achievement in aerial war. At this time he had already shot down 37 enemy planes.

Major Herbert Ihlefeld (1914-1995), Kommodore of JG 52, treasured the unique ability of an exceptional pilot. Ihlefeld was awarded the 9th Swords to the Oak Leaves on April 24, 1942.

Pilots of JG 52 relax with a round of Skat between missions.

Soviet MiG 3 fighters. At least 20 planes of this type were shot down by Graf.

Staffelkapitän of 9./JG 52

After his 50th aerial victory on March 23, 1942, he became Staffelkapitän of 9./JG 52, known as the "Karaya Squad" in the history of German fighter flying. Under his leadership it produced a series of successful fighter pilots. In a unique run, he flew to the top of German fighters in the following months. Graf scored one victory after another and matured as an aerial warfare specialist. Within three weeks he scored 48 aerial victories (his 61st to 108th), including six each on April 30 and May 13, seven each on May 2 and 8, and eight on May 14, 1942 (his 97th to 104th). His Squadron Kommodore at that time, Herbert Ihlefeld (1914-1995), the 9th recipient of the Swords, valued the unique ability of this exceptional pilot. Graf's Commander, Hubertus von Bonin (1911-1943), who led III. Gruppe of JG 52 from October 1, 1941, to July 5, 1943, also knew that Graf was an exceptional fighter pilot and aerial battle strategist.

On May 3, 1942, the Wehrmacht report announced:

"*on the previous day on the eastern front, Leutnant Köppen Scored his 80th to 84th, Leutnant Graf his 70th to 76th, and Feldwebel Steinbatz his 44th to 49th aerial victories.*"

On May 14, 1942, Graf had already been able to report his 100th aerial victory as the seventh fighter pilot to do so. In all, he shot down eight MiG 3 planes, totaling 104 kills. For this he became the 40th Luftwaffe member and first Reserve officer to receive the 93rd Oak Leaves on May 17, 1942. Only two days later, after his 105th aerial victory, which he scored in the Kharkov area on 15 May, he was awarded the 11th Swords to the Knight's Cross with Oak Leaves and was promoted to Oberleutnant of the Reserve.

On May 24, 1942, Graf, along with Leutnant Adolf Dickfeld (born 1910), flew to the Führer's "Wolf's Den" headquarters, where he was to be decorated with the Oak Leaves with Swords and Dickfeld the 94th Oak Leaves by the Supreme Commander. Then he began a home furlough, became one of the most photographed personalities, and was "passed around" for talks and visits.

On June 15, 1942, Graf's comrade Leopold Steinbatz was shot down. Graf, who was still on furlough at the time, learned of this from a newspaper article in Vienna. His loyal colleague and companion in countless aerial battles was shot down by Russian anti-aircraft fire near Woltschansk, beyond the front, after his 99th aerial victory. Oberfeldwebel Steinbatz was posthumously awarded the 14th Swords and promoted to Leutnant.

Graf returned to the front and the battle went on. For Graf there were further missions and further victories. Over the infantry battlefields and the enemy hinterlands he was able between 12 August and 3 September to score a total of 39 kills.

In the advance to Stalingrad, Graf volunteered for the "Stalingrad Battle Group" and flew under the command of Hauptmann Wolf-Dietrich Wilcke (1913-1944, 23rd Swords on 12/23/1942). Here Graf topped all that he had done before. It began with four kills (his 112th to 115th) on August 13, 1942, and his 140th opponent fell on 30 August. Flying to the limits of physical and mental ability, he shot down 62 enemies in August and September. On September 4, 1942, a Yak-1 became his 150th victim.

Jagdgeschwader 52

Emblem of the 9th Staffel
"Karaya Squad"

On March 24, 1942, Oberleutnant Graf became the Staffelkapitän of 9./JG 52, the "Karaya Squad". He was also to lead it in the fighting around Stalingrad. This is the squadron's emblem.

Nothing shows the toughness of this fighting more than the fact that his "Yellow 1", with which he had scored 75 aerial victories, showed over 100 bullet holes in its fuselage at the end. On 15 September he was hit in the cabin by a cannon shell, on 16 September his plane took 30 shots, on 19 September an anti-aircraft hit in the wing, and on the evening of the same day half of his rudder was shot away.

Then the group was moved to Pitomnik airfield near Stalingrad. After his 172nd kill on September 16, 1942, he was awarded the Diamonds to the Oak Leaves. As the propaganda machine became aware of him, he became one of the most often-photographed and best-known soldiers in the war. This was not always an advantage for him. Graf would not be limited by what he had achieved, but kept flying up to four missions daily and allowed himself no rest.

On May 14, 1942, Leutnart Graf was able to report his 100th aerial victory as the 7th pilot to do so, for which he became the 40th Luftwaffe member and first Reserve officer to be awarded the 93rd Oak Leaves on May 17, 1942. In all, he shot down eight MiG 3s that day for a total of 104 aerial victories.

Only one day later he scored his 105th kill, for which he received the 11th swords to the Knight's Cross with Oak Leaves and was promoted to Oberleutnant of the Reserve.

On July 1, 1942, Feldwebel Grislawski was honored with the Knight's Cross after 43 kills.

On May 24, 1942, Graf flew with Leutnant Adolf Dickfeld (born 1910), pilot in 7./JG 52, to the Führer's "Wolf's Den" headquarters, where he was awarded the Oak Leaves with Swords and Dickfeld received the 94th Oak Leaves, presented by the Supreme Commander.

Adolf Dickfeld (right) and Hermann Graf visited Oberst Angermund in the Berlin Air Office during their stay in Berlin after Graf was awarded the Oak Leaves and Swords.

Sergeant-Major Ernst Süss. In the wake of Hermann Graf, he soon ranked among the aces of the "Karaya Squad". After 50 aerial victories he was awarded the Knight's Cross on September 4, 1942. Promoted to officer's rank, Graf summoned him to JG 50. Süss fell south of Oldenburg on December 20, 1943, as Oberleutnant and Staffelkapitän of 9./JG 11 when he was shot by American fighters while hanging from his parachute.

Planes of JG 52 at Gomel airfield in Russia.

Feldwebel Leopold Steinbatz, comrade-in-arms of Hermann Graf, joined KG 52 with Graf in November 1940 and became his wingman. After 42 aerial victories he was awarded the Knight's Cross on September 14, 1942.

Summer 1941: "Poldi" Steinbatz with ground crewmen of his "Yellow 8".

A shot-down Il-2 "Sturmovik".

German soldiers examine a shot-down I-16 "Rata".

With the Yak-9, a strong fighter was available to the Soviet armed forces.

On September 21, 1941, the fighting for the peninsula of Crimea, in the Black Sea, began. It was to last until the Russian forces had been defeated on July 4, 1942. Here Graf encountered bitter opponents. The picture shows Yak-9 planes in action over Crimea.

In the advance toward Stalingrad, Graf volunteered for the "Stalingrad Battle Group" and flew under the command of Hauptmann Wolf-Dietrich Wilcke (1913-1944, 23rd Swords on 12/23/1942).

After his promotion to Hauptmann, in the late summer of 1942 Graf flew over Stalingrad again after his missions over the peninsula of Crimea.

September 1942, Pitomnik airfield near Stalingrad: Graf (center) with pilots of the 9./JG 52 during a break in the action. At left is Oberfeldwebel Süss and second from right is Oberfeldwebel Füllgrabe.

Pitomnik airfield, just outside Stalingrad, from which Graf's squad flew missions over Stalingrad to support the Army units.

Gumrak airfield in Stalingrad. Here Graf and his squad supported the units of the 6th Army in their fight for the city on the Volga.

On the horizon is Gumrak airfield.

A shot-down Me 109 in Stalingrad.

The destruction in southern Stalingrad.

Grislawski, Füllgrabe, and Gratz (left to right) during the Stalingrad action.

The destruction in Stalingrad from a different perspective, with the destroyed Bf 109 from the previous page.

The destruction of Stalingrad as seen from the air.

The rudder of Graf's "Yellow 1" at Kharkov-Rogan airfield on May 14, 1942. To date 104 kills had been recorded.

Only two days later, on May 20, 1942, Graf shot down a Pe-2 bomber and was decorated with the Swords to the Oak Leaves. Group Commander von Bonin wishes the "new" Swords-bearer luck on his return to the squadron.

May 1942, Crimea, Russia: The rudder of Graf's Bf 109 F-4 after 108 kills.

Left: May 1942. 9./JG 52 on a mission over Crimea. Hermann Graf took this picture from his cockpit. The yellow recognition stripe on Graf's wing is easy to see.

An Ilyushin Il-2 "Sturmovik". Eleven of these planes fell victim to Graf's weapons. Alfred Grislawski was a specialist in fighting these planes. He showed Erich Hartmann, among others, where they were vulnerable.

A unique picture made by Graf during a flight over the Caucasus. At right is the reflex visor of his Me 109, and ahead of him to the left are three Russian fighters, two of which he was soon able to shoot down.

Graf climbs from his plane after returning from a successful mission.

Graf was a more and more desired subject of photographs. Here he faces the camera with a Luftwaffe Feldwebel and an Army official.

The Captain of 9./JG 52, Hermann Graf, scored his 172nd aerial victory near Stalingrad on September 15, 1942, and is greeted jubilantly by his men.

First Fighter Pilot with 200 Aerial Victories

When he became the world's first pilot to shoot down 172 enemies on September 9, 1942, Graf finally received the 5th Diamonds to the Knight's Cross with Oak Leaves and Swords. Within 235 days the officer had been decorated with all the medals of bravery and had become the hero of the Luftwaffe. On the very next day he shot down five more planes. In the late summer of 1942 Graf, having flown missions over the peninsula of Crimea, once again flew over Stalingrad. There Graf experienced the toughness of the fighting and the unbroken fighting spirit of some Soviet fighter pilots with his own body.

His squad was the last to hold out in the pocket of Stalingrad, and many soldiers lost hope when Graf's voice resounded from the air on the army radio:

"Farewell, Comrades of Stalingrad!—Karaya One signs out—on higher command!"

On September 23, 1942, he was able to score ten aerial victories (his 188th to 197th), and on 26 September he became the first fighter pilot to exceed the score of 200 planes (his 200th to 202nd) shot down. He had amassed this total in only 13 months. On October 1, 1942, he was promoted to Major. In three years he had risen from Feldwebel to Major. In 1942 he was also taken into the active officer corps.

Now Graf was forbidden to fly and could work more intensively on the "Red Hunters" Luftwaffe soccer team he had founded, to which, among others, Fritz Walter belonged.

By shooting down a LaGG 3 fighter on September 15, 1942, Hermann Graf scored his 172nd aerial victory. He was able to shoot down twenty planes of this type in all.

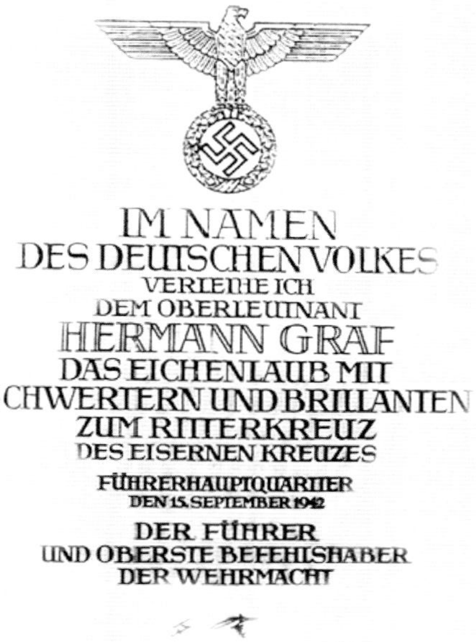

IM NAMEN
DES DEUTSCHEN VOLKES
VERLEIHE ICH
DEM OBERLEUTNANT
HERMANN GRAF
DAS EICHENLAUB MIT
SCHWERTERN UND BRILLANTEN
ZUM RITTERKREUZ
DES EISERNEN KREUZES
FÜHRERHAUPTQUARTIER
DEN 15. SEPTEMBER 1942
DER FÜHRER
UND OBERSTE BEFEHLSHABER
DER WEHRMACHT

On September 15, 1942, Hermann Graf became the 5th fighter pilot, as well as the 5th Army soldier, to be decorated with the Oak Leaves with Swords and Diamonds to the Knight's Cross. Here is the award certificate, with the text printed in gold.

On September 15, 1942, Hermann Graf as Staffelkapitän in 9./JG 52 scored his 172nd aerial victory near Stalingrad and was decorated with the Diamonds to the Knight's Cross with Oak Leaves and Swords, and on 1 October he was promoted to Major.

On September 25, 1942, Graf scored his 198th and 199th kills, shooting down two La-5 planes.

The Führer's "Wolf's Den" headquarters, where the Oak Leaves and Swords are being awarded (from left to right) to Hermann Graf, Werner Baumbach (16th Swords as Hauptmann and Commander of I./JG 30), and Heinz Bär (1913-1957, 7th swords as Hauptmann and Staffelkapitän of I./JG 51 "Mölders") by Adolf Hitler.

On October 1, 1942, Graf was promoted to Major.

The Bf 109 G of Hermann Graf.

The Diamond-wearer visits his military comrades: Knight's Cross bearer Erich Vielwerth, right (1912-1997, Knight's Cross as Oberfeldwebel and Platoon Leader in I./Inf/Reg. 87 (mot.) on 10./18/1041); and Pour-le-Merite bearer Siegfried Rungs (1884-1945, Knight's Cross as Oberst and Commander of Inf. Reg. 297) on 12/20/1941.

On November 1, 1942, Oberstleutnant Dietrich Hrabak (1914-1995) succeeded the retiring Kommodore Herbert Ihlefeld.

From left to right: Grislawski, Graf, Füllgrabe and Süss, the aces of the "Karaya Squad".

Leutnant Grislawski and young Erich Hartmann. Grislawski showed Hartmann where the "Stormoviks" were vulnerable. At left is Edmund "Paule" Rossmann (Knight's Cross on 3/19/1942).

Diamond bearer Graf as a guest of Reichsmarschall Hermann Göring.

During his home furlough, Graf had the chance to examine the Me 262 while it was being developed. Here he sits in the cockpit of a test model.

After a demonstration flight with an Me 109.

The Luftwaffe journal *Der Adler* also reported on Graf's visit to Messerschmitt.

Hermann Graf and Prof. Willy Messerschmitt.

Arriving in his home town, Graf is warmly greeted at the Engen railroad station.

Hermann Graf and his mother.

He signs the Golden Book of the City of Engen.

Graf signs the Golden Book of the City of Munich.

Hermann Graf and Major Werner Bradel (1911-1943), Kommodore of JG 2 "Holzhammer", during the visit of flying units to the west. Bradel received the Knight's Cross on September 17, 1941, as Hauptmann and Staffelkapitän in KG 2.

Two successful fighter pilots and idols of young people: Graf and the later Oberstleutnant Egon Mayer (1917-1944).

The Comrades-in-Arms

After 75 aerial victories, Oberfeldwebel Steinbatz was decorated with the 96th Oak Leaves to the Knight's Cross. On June 15, 1942, after his 99th aerial victory, Leopold Steinbatz fell victim to anti-aircraft fire near Woltschansk, in the southern sector of the eastern front. He was posthumously awarded the 14th Swords and promoted to Leutnant. He was the only NCO who received this high honor.

Leopold Steinbatz, the only Unteroffizier with the Swords

Leopold Steinbatz was born in Vienna on October 25, 1918. "Bazi" entered the Pilot Training Regiment of the Austrian Army in 1937. His flight training began in August 1939.

In November 1940 he joined the 9th Staffel of JG 52 and became a wingman to Hermann Graf. During the Balkan campaign and the Cretan operation he stood out in successful low-level raids. On August 4, 1941, he scored his first aerial victory on the eastern front. In the wake of his squad leader, he quickly became an ace in his service arm. On November 29, 1941, he scored his 25th aerial victory, and on December 27, 1941, his 32nd. On December 8, 1941, he received the Cup of Honor for special achievement in aerial war. After his 42nd kill on January 8, 1942, at the rank of Feldwebel he received the Knight's Cross. On January 25, 1942, he was also awarded the German Cross in Gold, for which he had previously been nominated. But because of his quick success, the Knight's Cross was awarded to him sooner.

At the end of April 1942, after a well-earned home furlough, he returned to the front and performed splendidly again, quickly shooting down six enemies (his 44th to 49th). On May 5, 1942, his 50th and 51st victims fell to him, and on May 8, 1942, he was able to record seven aerial victories. These were opponents 52 to 58. Steinbatz scored his 75th aerial victory on May 20, 1942, and was able to defeat four enemies each on June 1 and 2, 1942 (numbers 84 to 91), for which he was, as an Oberfeldwebel, decorated with the 96th Oak Leaves.

Flying to exhaustion, he allowed himself only a brief pause, for he absolutely wanted to achieve his 100th kill before taking a well-earned furlough. On June 11, 1942, he reported his 95th aerial victory, and on 15 June his 97th to 99th kills, but on his return flight he was hit by anti-aircraft fire and crashed over a wooded area northwest of Schtebelaino near Woltschansk, in the Soviet Union, where he presumably died (Bf 109 F-4, 13357, "Yellow 2"). Since that day Leopold Steinbatz, who had flown some 300 missions successfully, has been listed as missing.

He was posthumously honored with the Swords to the Oak Leaves and also promoted to Leutnant. He was the only Unteroffizier who earned this high honor.

Heinrich Füllgrabe, Flying Ace in Hermann Graf's Wake

Heinrich Fellgrabe, born in Witzenhausen, Hesse, on July 26, 1916, was an Unteroffizier in the 9th Staffel of JG 52 beginning in the spring of 1941. His career as a fighter pilot is closely linked with the rise of Hermann Graf, in whose famed "Karaya Squad" he steadily rose higher. On February 25, 1942, he received the German Cross in Gold, and on March 30, 1942, the Cup of Honor for special achievement in the air war. Most of his aerial victories were won in the summer of 1942. After 52 kills he was awarded the Knight's Cross as an Oberfeldwebel on October 2, 1942. In the spring of 1943 he returned to his old unit after a long pause and raised his score to 65. In June 1943 Graf called him to JG 50;

Heinrich Füllgrabe (1916-1945) came to 9./JG 52 as an Unteroffizier in the spring of 1941. His career as a fighter pilot is closely linked with Hermann Graf. He scored most of his aerial victories in the summer of 1942. After 52 kills he was awarded the Knight's Cross as an Oberfeldwebel on October 2, 1942. On January 30, 1945, he was shot down fatally by Russian anti-aircraft fire during a low-level attack on Soviet tanks.

as of December 1943 he became a flight instructor in Replacement Group East. When Hermann Graf became Kommodore of JG 52, he called Füllgrabe to the squadron's staff at the end of 1944. On January 30, 1945, his plane (Bf 109 G-14, works number 511012, "Green 2") was hit fatally by Russian anti-aircraft fire in a low-level attack on Soviet tanks. Before his death, Oberleutnant Heinrich Füllgrabe had won 67 aerial victories in the east.

On December 1, 1942, Grislawski was promoted to Lieutenant. The joy is obviously great.

Alfred Grislawski, Ranking 51 on the List of the Best with 133 Aerial Victories

Alfred Grislawski was born in Wanne-Eickel, in the Ruhr district, on February 11, 1919. He joined the 9th Staffel of JG 52 in Romania in November 1940, and took part in the Balkan campaign and Cretan operation. He was one of Hermann Graf's best students and, in his wake, slowly made his way upward. On September 1, 1941, he scored his first aerial victory, and scored about ten by the end of 1941. On May 30, 1942, he was honored with the Cup of Honor, was especially successful in May and June 1942, and after 43 aerial victories, as a Feldwebel was awarded the Knight's Cross on July 1, 1942. He was ordered to Replacement Group East for several months as a flight instructor. In October 1942 he returned to the eastern front and joined the 7th Staffel of JG 52. On November 6, 1942, he scored his 63rd to 68th kills; on December 12, 1942, his 79th to 82nd; and was promoted to Leutnant. On February 3, 1943, he shot down his 93rd opponent, his 100th on April 27, 1943, and his 108th and 109th on June 3, 1943. The next day he was wounded in the explosion of a land mine. After his recovery Graf called him to his special unit (JG South, later JG 50), where on August 17, 1943, he shot down his first two four-engine U.S. planes. On November 6, 1943, he was named Staffelkapitän of the 1st Staffel of JG 1. On January 24, 1944, Alfred Grislawski was wounded in an air battle (FW 190 A-7, works number 430167, "White 1"). After he recovered he became Staffelkapitän of the 8th Staffel of JG 1 on March 13, 1944. His ruthless action against four-engine U.S. planes was honored on April 11, 1944, with the conferring of the 446th Oak Leaves. He was a Hauptmann at that time and had scored about 122 aerial victories. At the end of July 1944 he became the Staffelkapitän of 11./JG 53. On September 26, 1944, he was badly wounded in an aerial battle near Münster and parachuted out. After the war Grislawski returned to his home town and worked successfully as a master artisan until he retired. The rudder of one of his Me 109s, showing 114 scores from his missions, survived the war, and he kept it in his cellar for years before donating it not many years ago to the Air Travel Museum in Hannover-Laatzen, where it found a worthy home. On March 19, 2003, he died in his home town of Wanne-Eickel as the last living ace of the "Karaya Squad" of JG 52.

New Tasks

Early in 1943 Graf was wounded in the arm and ordered to Germany for propaganda appearances. The "Hero of Stalingrad" was to be seen at numerous soccer games then, and in almost all front-page pictures. After more than two years of constant action, this was his first real recovery time. During the combat in the east, Graf had had no spare time for his favorite sport, soccer. He himself was an enthusiastic and above-average amateur goalie. Over time Graf used his popularity and his rank to organize a renowned and also very well-manned soccer team in his squadron. Many famous pre- and postwar soccer players belonged to this team, sarcastically called "The Red Hunters". When the German Soccer League complained that Graf often had good soccer players transferred to his squadron, Reichsmarschall Göring replied coolly, "*As long as he is so successful, he can play soccer as much as he wants.*"

At this time a friendship that outlasted everything began. Sepp Herberger, then the Reich coach, and Hermann Graf became close friends. After the war this friendship remained firm, and it was Herberger who helped Graf, coming home after imprisonment, to get a start in civilian life. Graf also became close friends with Fritz Walter, the later honorary leader of the German National Team and Captain of the German Eleven during the 1956 World Championship games in Switzerland.

After his recovery, Graf was named Commander of Fighter Replacement Group East in southern France. In March 1943 the Major was assigned to develop a high-level fighter group to fight against "Mosquitoes" (Fighter Group South), from which JG 50 was later formed, and which he later commanded in defending the Reich against the streams of American bombers. The second high-altitude squadron of the Luftwaffe was then commanded by Graf's former Kommodore, Oberstleutnant Ihlefeld.

A friendship that outlasted the war: Graf and Sepp Herberger, then the Reich coach.

Hermann Graf played goalie on the Luftwaffe soccer team, "The Red Hunters".

Thus, the Diamond-holder of the squad had risen to be a squadron leader without ever having commanded a front fighter unit. He shot down a "Mosquito" over Groningen, plus two Boeing B-17s (his 204th and 205th) on September 6, 1943.

On December 16, 1943, Hermann Graf became Kommodore of JG 11. Although he flew relatively seldom because of his irreplaceable activity as Squadron Commander, he was able to shoot down ten U.S. bombers at that time.

JG 11 was on the so-called "Road of the Bombers", the main approach route of the heavy American four-engine bombers. Graf's I. Gruppe was led by the successful bomber-killer Major Rolf Hermichen (born

Hermann Graf (center) as goalie in Hannover in 1943 with Fritz Walter (right). At left, in a Navy uniform, is national player Paul Janes of Fortuna Düsseldorf.

Hermann Graf was an enthusiastic soccer player. He founded the Luftwaffe soccer team "The Red Hunters", on which he played goalie.

On March 6, 1943, Major Günther Rall (born 1918) took over as Kommandeur of III. Gruppe from the late Major von Bonin. With 275 aerial victories, Rall became the third most successful fighter pilot in history. On September 12, 1943, he received the 34th Swords to the Oak Leaves.

Summer 1943, from left to right: Günther Rall, Graf, and Adalbert Sommer.

In March 1943 Graf was empowered to organize a high-altitude fighter group to fight "Mosquitoes". The "Mosquito", also nicknamed the "Wooden Wonder", was extremely fast and, because of their light wooden structure, could fly extremely high. In June 1943 Graf was able to shoot down a "Mosquito".

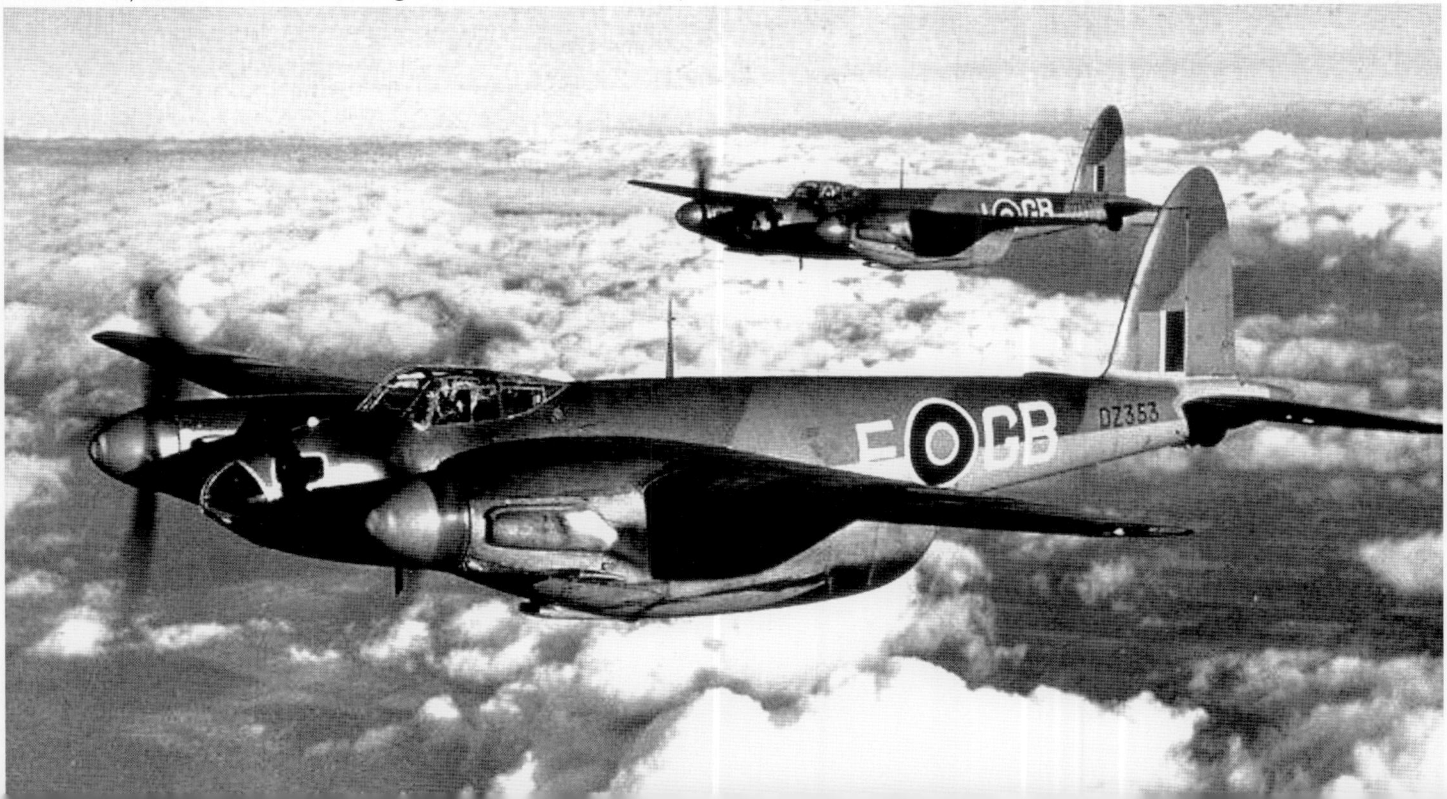

In April 1943 Graf took command of Fighter Replacement Group East. By that time he was the first German fighter pilot who had shot down 200 opponents in air combat.

April 1943: Several weeks of the toughest action as a fighter pilot in surrounded Stalingrad are suitably honored. Hermann Graf, Kommandeur of Replacement Group East, decorates Feldwebel Kurt Ebner (1920-1975) with the Knight's Cross conferred on April 7, 1942. Ebner finished the war as an Oberleutnant and Staffelkapitän in JG 11.

1918), and III. Gruppe by Swords-bearer Major Anton Hackl (1915-1984). On March 29, 1944, Graf ran out of ammunition during an air fight for victory over two "Flying Fortresses". Attacked by several escort fighters, Graf used his only remaining chance, faced one of the American "Mustangs", and rammed his opponent. He was badly wounded, but was able to get out of his plane (Bf 109 G-6, works number 26020, "Black Angle") by parachute at the right time, and was taken to a hospital. This unconventional victory was the last of his total of 212 confirmed kills. The high price for it was six months of hospital and recovery time—after which the Diamond-holder was strictly forbidden to fly. JG 11 was taken over by Oberstleutnant Günther Specht (1914-1945), a Knight's Cross bearer who was awarded the Oak Leaves after his death in January 1945.

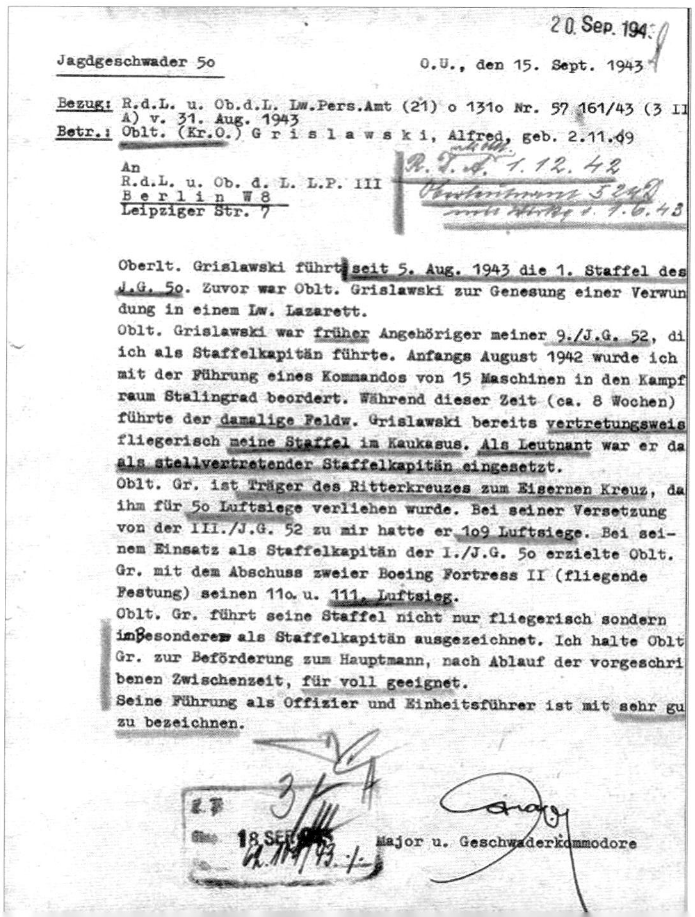

20. Sep. 194

Jagdgeschwader 5o O.U., den 15. Sept. 1943

Bezug: R.d.L. u. Ob.d.L. Lw.Pers.Amt (21) o 131o Nr. 57 161/43 (3 II A) v. 31. Aug. 1943
Betr.: Oblt. (Kr.O.) G r i s l a w s k i, Alfred, geb. 2.11.19

An
R.d.L. u. Ob. d. L. L.P. III
B e r l i n W 8
Leipziger Str. 7

R.D.A. 1.12.42

Oberlt. Grislawski führt seit 5. Aug. 1943 die 1. Staffel des J.G. 5o. Zuvor war Oblt. Grislawski zur Genesung einer Verwundung in einem Lw. Lazarett.
Oblt. Grislawski war früher Angehöriger meiner 9./J.G. 52, di[e] ich als Staffelkapitän führte. Anfangs August 1942 wurde ich mit der Führung eines Kommandos von 15 Maschinen in den Kampfraum Stalingrad beordert. Während dieser Zeit (ca. 8 Wochen) führte der damalige Feldw. Grislawski bereits vertretungsweis[e] fliegerisch meine Staffel im Kaukasus. Als Leutnant war er da als stellvertretender Staffelkapitän eingesetzt.
Oblt. Gr. ist Träger des Ritterkreuzes zum Eisernen Kreuz, da[s] ihm für 5o Luftsiege verliehen wurde. Bei seiner Versetzung von der III./J.G. 52 zu mir hatte er 1o9 Luftsiege. Bei seinem Einsatz als Staffelkapitän der I./J.G. 5o erzielte Oblt. Gr. mit dem Abschuss zweier Boeing Fortress II (fliegende Festung) seinen 11o. u. 111. Luftsieg.
Oblt. Gr. führt seine Staffel nicht nur fliegerisch sondern imßesonderem als Staffelkapitän ausgezeichnet. Ich halte Oblt Gr. zur Beförderung zum Hauptmann, nach Ablauf der vorgeschri[e]benen Zwischenzeit, für voll geeignet.
Seine Führung als Offizier und Einheitsführer ist mit sehr gu[t] zu bezeichnen.

18 SEP
Major u. Geschwaderkommodore

On September 15, 1943, Graf recommended the promotion of Alfred Grislawski to Hauptmann.

Two successful fighter pilots and idols of young people: Graf and the subsequent Oberstleutnant Egon Mayer (1917-1944), who was very successful in fighting against four-engine American bombers. Mayer, to whom the 51st Swords were awarded on March 21, 1944, died on the same day in an aerial battle near Montmedy after 102 aerial victories in the west, including 25 four-engine and two two-engine bombers.

Alfred Grislawski was promoted to Captain on October 1, 1943. He flew in Graf's JG 50 until the unit was disbanded. On November 6, 1943, he became the Staffelkapitän of I./JG I in Dortmund.

October 3, 1943, JG 50: Graf and Oberfeldwebel Füllgrabe in front of Graf's Bf 109 G-6 (Cannon Boat) "Red 1" with WGr 21 equipment. Here the dark red tulip design with yellow and white borders is easy to see.

October 3, 1943, JG 50. Hermann Graf's Bf 109 G-6. The spotty camouflage on the fuselage is easy to see, as is the sawtooth pattern on the wings. Graf rides his BMW "Commander's Cycle".

October 1943: Graf in the cabin of his Bf 109 G-6 "Red 1" of JG 50. Under the sill is the emblem of the "Red Hunters", which Graf used only on this plane. The symbol was applied to the port side by many pilots, but each emblem was different.

Graf at the tail of his (all-white) Me 109 G-6, with 205 kill symbols on the rudder. On the upper part are the initials HG, enclosed by the ribbon of the Knight's Cross with Oak Leaves and Swords, plus the number 172, the number of kills for which he received the Diamonds.

Grislawski's Bf 109 G-6, which also bears spot camouflage and the "Red Hunter" emblem. At left is Heinrich Füllgrabe.

Again we see the rudder of Graf's Me 109 G-6.

Grislawski's rudder was painted in the same scheme as Graf's.

Wiesbaden-Erbenheim: Graf, Grislawski and Füllgrabe (from left) wait for action.

Also at Wiesbaden-Erbenheim: Graf with Heinrich Füllgrabe.

Graf and Grislawski relax while with JG 50 in Wiesbaden-Erbenheim.

Graf and Grislawski with JG 50 in Wiesbaden-Erbenheim.

A B-17 formation over Germany.

Reichsmarschall Göring visits JG 50 in Wiesbaden-Erbenheim. At left in the picture is General Loerzer.

JG 11

JG 11 was established in Jever on April 1, 1943, from the I. and III. Gruppe of JG 1 and formed the basis of this new squadron as the I. and II. Gruppe, with the 10th and 11th Staffels. Equipped with the Focke-Wulf Fw 190 A and II. Gruppe with the Messerschmitt Me 109 G, it was enlarged in 1944 to three groups of four squads each. On December 16, 1943, Oberstleutnant Hermann Graf took over the leadership of the squadron, succeeding Kommodore Major Anton Mader (1913-1984).

In 1943 and 1944 the squadron flew missions in the Reich Airspace Defense under Luftwaffe Commander Berlin. In April 1944 Major Anton Hackl (1915-1984) succeeded Hermann Graf and took on the work of the Kommodore. After the Allied invasion of France it was subordinated to the 5th Fighter Division. In June 1944 the Staff and I. Gruppe moved to Le Mans; II. Gruppe remained with the 4th Fighter Division in Monsen-Chaussee. In September 1944 I. Gruppe was located in Gelnhausen and II. in Gymnich. III. Gruppe saw service in the east with Air Fleet 6 and was stationed in Dokudevo with Fighter Sector Leader 6 in June 1944. As of July 1944 in Radom and as of September in Nermakseiai, it saw service on the eastern front with Air Fleet 6 in 1945. On 5 February the staff was with II. Gruppe in Straussberg, I. Gruppe in Finow, and III. Gruppe in Neuhardenberg. Then the war ended for JG 11.

On November 16, 1943, Graf took command of JG 11 as its Kommodore, and was promoted to Oberstleutnant on May 1, 1944.

A B-17 formation unloads its deadly freight over Germany.

Front view of a four-engine American B-17 bomber. Hermann Graf was able to shoot down three of these "Flying Fortresses".

A Focke-Wulf Fw 190 daylight fighter of JG 11.

Kommodore of JG 52

Graf in "full regalia".

In October 1944 Oberstleutnant Graf returned to the eastern front and succeeded the legendary Oak-Leaf bearer Colonel Dietrich Hrabak (1914-1995) to lead his old squadron, JG 52, which was still in the southern sector of the eastern front. Along with Army units, the elite squadron moved farther and farther back to the west. In January 1945 the highly decorated Squadron Kommodore took part, along with Swords bearers Oberst Günther Lützow (1912-1945), Oberst Josef Priller (1915-1961), and Oberst Johannes Steinhoff (1913-1994) in the so-called "Mutiny of the Fighter Pilots" against the Supreme Commander of the Luftwaffe, Reichsmarschall Hermann Göring (1893-1946). Unlike many others, Hermann Graf remained unsuspected after its failure. In May Graf's pilots flew their last missions over Czechoslovakia. When the order to surrender arrived, Graf, now Oberst, had the last planes blown up and all other equipment destroyed.

JG 52, thanks to its outstanding pilots, became the most successful Luftwaffe unit. Along with such well known aces as Erich Hartmann (1922-1993) with 352 aerial victories, Gerhard Barkhorn (1919-1983) with 301, Günther Rall (born 1918) with 275, Wilhelm Batz (1916-1988) with 237, Helmut Lipfert (1916-1990) with 203, Walter Krupinski (1920-2000) with 197, Karl Gratz (1919-2002) with 138, and Adolf Dickfeld with 136, Graf with his more than 200 aerial victories contributed to the unforgettable fame of the squadron. In all, the pilots of the squadron scored no fewer than 10,800 confirmed aerial victories between 1939 and 1945. Seventy of them were decorated with the Knight's Cross or its higher degrees.

A Focke-Wulf Fw 190 G-3. Graf's squadron flew planes of this type in the defense of the Reich.

A band of American B-24 "Liberator" bombers flying to a new target. Three of these large bombers fell victim to Graf's weapons.

The Aces of JG 52 with more than 100 Aerial Victories

Name	Rank	Kills	Born/Died	Decorations
Hartmann, Erich	Major	352	1922-1993	RESB
Barkhorn, Gerhard	Major	301	1919-1993	RES
Rall, Günther	Major	275	1918	RES
Batz, Wilhelm	Major	237	1916-1988	RES
Graf, Hermann	Oberst	212	1912-1988	RESB
Lipfert, Helmut	Hauptmann	203	1916-1990	RE
Krupinski, Walter	Hauptmann	197	1920-2000	RE
Steinhoff, Johannes	Oberst	178	1913-1994	RES
Schmidt, Heinz	Hauptmann	173	1920-1943	RE
Sturm, Heinrich	Hauptmann	158	1920-1944	R
Duettmann, Peter	Leutnant	150	1923-2001	R
Gratz, Karl	Leutnant	138	1919-2002	R
Trenkel, Rudolf	Hauptmann	138	1918-	R
Wolfrum, Walter	Oberleutnant	137	1923	R
Foennekold, Otto	Oberleutnant	136	1920-1944	R
Waldmann, Hans	Oberleutnant	134	1922-1945	R
Grislawski, Alfred	Hauptmann	133	1919-2003	RE
Schall, Franz	Hauptmann	133	1918-1945	R
Wiese, Johannes	Major	133	1915-1991	RE
Borchers, Adolf	Major	132	1913	R
Dickfeld, Adolf	Oberst	132	1910	RE
Ihlefeld, Herbert	Oberst	132	1914-1995	RES
Hoffmann, Gerhard	Leutnant	130	1919-1945	R
Zwernemann, Josef	Oberleutnant	126	1916-1944	RE
Hrabak, Dieter	Oberst	125	1914-1995	RE
Wachowiak, Friedrich	Leutnant	120	1920-1944	R
Obleser, Friedrich	Oberleutnant	120	1923	R
Birkner, Hans-Joachim	Leutnant	117	1921-1944	R
Dammers, Hans	Leutnant	117	1918	R
Korts, Berthold	Leutnant	113	1912-1943	R
Woidich, Franz	Oberleutnant	110	1921	R
Sachsenberg, Heinz	Leutnant	104	1922-1951	R
Miethig, Rudolf	Hauptmann	101	1921-1943	R

R = Knight's Cross
RE = R with Oak Leaves
RES = R with E and Swords
RESB = R with Oak Leaves, Swords and Diamonds

Visibly exhausted after service in homeland defense.

An American P-47 "Thunderbolt". Used as escorts of American four-engine bombers, they shot down several German fighters.

A daily scene in 1944-45: Vapor trails in the sky over Germany. A squadron of B-17 "Flying Fortresses" flies toward their next target.

Confirmed Kills of Hermann Graf

#	Date	Time	Type	Unit	Place, Notes
1	8/4/1941	6:20	I-16	9./JG 52	1 km SE Kiev
2	8/5/1041	6:20	I-16	9./JG 52	3 km SW Kiev
3	8/11/1941	14:35	MiG-3	9./JG 52	2 km E Kanev
4	8/30/1941	8:40	DB-3	9./JG 52	60 km NE Dnepropetrovsk
5	9/8/1941	18:23	I-16	9./JG 52	25-30km E Kremenchug
6	9/13/1941	10:46	Yak-1	9./JG 52	15 km NW Perekop
7	9/24/1941	12:10	DB-3	9./JG 52	Balakliya
8	9/27/1941	14:22	DB-3	9./JG 52	50 km W Kharkov
9	10/3/1941	17:00	Yak-1	9./JG 52	10 km E Kharkov
10	10/3/1941	17:05	I-16	9./JG 52	East of Kharkov
11	10/11/1941	7:10	SB-2	9./JG 52	10 km E Lozovaka
12	10/11/1941	7:15	I-153	9./JG 52	20 km E Lozovaya
13	10/14/1941	16:10	Yak-1	9./JG 52	10 km N Valki
14	10/14/1941	16:13	Yak-1	9./JG 52	10 km N Valki
15	10/24/1941	12:50	MiG-3	9./JG 52	Boysovka
16	10/24/1941	12:52	Mig-3	9./JG 52	Boysovka
17	10/25/1941	15:21	Mig-3	9./JG 52	Over Aibar (Yak-1 0f 32.IAP VVS-Chf, Pilot Michail Avdevyev, 17 kills)
18	10/27/1941	15:38	MiG-3	9./KG 52	10 km S Juschno
19	10/28/1941	10:02	MiG-3	9./KG 52	SE Aibar
20	10/28/1941	10:03	R-5	9./KG 52	SE Aibar
21	11/1/1941	16:15	MiG-3	9./JG 52	N Sevastopol
22	11/8/1941	11:58	MiG-3	9./JG 52	S Rostov
23	11/9/1941	14:35	I-16	9./JG 52	10 km E Schachti
24	11/11/1941	14:35	MiG-3	9./JG 52	N Roveniki
25	11/17/1941	14:38	I-16	9./JG 52	10 km E Rostov
26	11/20/1941	13:52	Su-2	9./JG 52	20 km NE Agrafenovka
27	11/23/1941	13:36	Il-2	9./JG 52	S Rostov
28	11/29/1941	10:21	I-16	9./JG 52	10 km NE Rostov
29	11/29/1941	10:27	DB-3	9./JG 52	ENE Rostov
30	11/29/1941	13:07	I-16	9./JG 52	S Bataisk
31	12/2/1941	12:19	I-16	9./JG 52	20 km S Taganrog
32	12/6/1941	12:52	Il-2	9./JG 52	E Lysogorskaya
33	12/6/1941	14:25	I-16	9./JG 52	W Azov
34	12/6/1941	14:32	I-16	9./JG 52	E Azov
35	12/8/1941	9:43	I-5	9./JG 52	20 km E Taganrog
36	12/8/1941	9:44	I-5	9./JG 52	25 km E Taganrog
37	12/8/1941	9:52	I-16	9./JG 52	SW Rabovka
38	12/27/1941	12:01	I-16	9./JG 52	Don Delta 30 km E Taganrog
39	12/27/1941	12:05	I-16	9./JG 52	10 km E Azov
40	12/27/1941	14:25	I-16	9./JG 52	NE Golodayevka
41	12/27/1941	14:30	SB-2	9./JG 52	NE Golodayevka
42	12/28/1941	13:32	Yak-1	9./JG 52	20 km SW Taganrog

#	Date	Time	Plane	Unit	Place, Notes
43	1/7/1942	14:50	I-16	9./JG 52	Sansnoye
44	1/7/1942	14:55	I-16	9./JG 52	Novaya Slobodka
45	1/8/1942	11:25	E/a	9./JG 52	E Prilepiy
46	1/25/1942	15:42	I-16	9./JG 52	10 km E Izyum
47	2/3/1942	9:35	Su-2	9./JG 52	Nuvo
48	3/23/1942	13:06	Yak-1	9,.JG 52	8 km SE Gniliza
49	3/23/1942	13:14	Yak-1	9./JG 52	3 km SE Burluk
50	3/23/1942	17:26	Su-2	9./JG 52	E Kotovka
51	3/25/1942	6:25	Yak-1	9./JG 52	15 km E Stary Saltov
52	3/27/1942	10:11	Yak-1	9./JG 52	15 km E Volchansk
53	3/27/1942	17:18	MiG-3	9./JG 52	10 km NE Burluk
54	3/28/1942	5:53	I-16	9./JG 52	3 km W Burluk
55	3/28/1942	6:18	Yak-1	9./JG 52	3 km W Kotovka
56	3/28/1942	17:08	MiG-3	9./JG 52	5 km E Saltov
57	3/28/1942	17:41	I-16	9./JG 52	Near Gniliza
58	3/30/1942	12:05	MiG-3	9./JG 52	15 km W Burluk
59	4/6/1942	6:02	I-16	9./JG 52	2 lm NE Staryi Saltov
60	4/6/1942	6:04	I-16	9./JG 52	10 km E Staryi Saltov
61	4/29/1942		Yak-1?	9./JG 52	Kerch
62	4/29/1942		Yak-1?	9./JG 52	Kerch
63	4/29/1942		Yak-1?	9./JG 52	Kerch
64	4/30/1942		E/a	9./JG 52	Kerch
65	4/30/1942		E/a	9./JG 52	Kerch
66	4/30/1942		E/a	9./JG 52	Kerch
67	4/30/1942	16:42	E/a	9./JG 52	Kerch
68	4/30/1942	16:47	E/a	9./JG 52	Kerch
69	4/30/1942	16:50	E/a	9./JG 52	Kerch
70	5/2/1942	4:00	I-16	9./JG 62	Kerch
71	5/2/1952	4:00	I-16	9./JG 52	Kerch
72	5/2/1942	4:00	I-16	9./JG 52	Kerch
73	5/2/1942	11:15	I-153	9./JG 52	Kerch
74	5/2/1942	11:15	E/a	9./JG 52	Kerch
75	5/2/1942		E/a	9./JG 52	Kerch
76	5/2/1942		E/a	9./JG 52	Kerch
77	5/3/1942		E/a	9./JG 52	Crimea
78	5/5/1942		E/a	9./JG 52	Crimea
79	5/8/1942		MiG-3	9./JG 52	Crimea
80	5/8/1942	10:05	Mig-3	9./JG 52	Crimea
81	5/8/1942	11:02	E/a	9./JG 52	Crimea
82	5/8/1942	11:07	E/a	9./JG 52	Crimea
83	5/8/1942		I-16	9./JG 52	Kerch
84	5/8/1942	13:32	E/a	9./JG 52	Kerch
85	5/8/1942	17:28	MiG-3	9./KG 52	Crimea

Confirmed Kills of Hermann Graf

#	Date	Time	Plane	Unit	Place, Notes
86	5/9/1942		E/a	9./JG 52	Crimea
87	5/9/1942		E/a	9./JG 52	Crimea
88	5/11/1942		I-16	9./JG 52	Kerch
89	5/11/1942		I-16	9./JG 52	Kerch
90	5/12/1942		E/a	9./JG 52	Kharkov-Rogan
91	5/13/1942		E/a	9./JG 52	Kharkov area
92	5/13/1942		E/a	9./JG 52	Kharkov area
93	5/13/1942		E/a	9./JG 52	Kharkov area
94	5/13/1942		E/a	9./JG 52	Kharkov area
95	5/13/1942		E/a	9./JG 52	Kharkov area
96	5/13/1942		E/a	9./JG 52	Kharkov area
97	5/14/1942		E/a	9,.JG 52	Kharkov area
98	5/14/1942		E/a	9./JG 52	Kharkov area
99	5/14/1942		E/a	9./JG 52	Kharkov area
100	5/14/1942		MiG-3	9./JG 52	Staryi-Saltov-Kotovka
101	5/14/1942	16:45	MiG-3	9./JG 52	Staryi-Saltov-Kotovka
102	5/14/1942	16:45	MiG-3	9./JG 52	Staryi-Saltov-Kotovka
103	5/14/1942	16:45	MiG-3	9./JG 52	Staryi-Saltov-Kotovka
104	5/14/1942	16:45	MiG-3	9./JG 52	Staryi-Saltov-Kotovka
105	5/15/1942		E/a	9./JG 52	Kharkov area
106	5/20/1942	17:37	Pe-3	9./JG 52	Kharkov area
107	5/21/1942		MiG-3	9./JG 52	
108	5/23/1942	16:28	I-16	9./JG 52	Kharkov area
109	6/30/1942		E/a	9./JG 52	Kharkov-Rogan
110	6/30/1942		E/a	9./JG 52	Kharkov
111	6/30/1942		E/a	9./JG 52	Kharkov
112	8/3/1942	18:30	Il-2	9./JG 52	Map Square 06 670
113	8/5/1942	9:37	LaGG-3	9./JG 52	Map Square 06 760
114	8/12/1942	14:32	Yak-1	9./JG 52	Map Square 86 754
115	8/13/1942	15:32	I-16	9./JG 52	Map Square 85 123
116	8/14/1942	10:14	I-16	9./JG 52	Map Square 95 112
117	8/14/1942	10:20	I-16	9./JG 52	Map Square 95 113
118	8/14/1942	13:37	Yak-1	9./JG 52	Map Square 85 263
119	8/14/1942	13:52	Hurricane	9./JG 52	Map Square 85 224
120	8/14/1942	13:57	LaGG-3	9./JG 52	Map Square 85 241
121	8/15/1942	16:41	Yak-1	9./JG 52	Map Square 95 174
122	8/16/1942	16:54	I-16	9./JG 52	Map Square 85 314
123	8/17/1942	11:42	I-153	9./JG 52	Map Square 85 423
124	8/17/1942	15:36	I-153	9./JG 52	Map Square 85 433
125	8/17/1942	15:41	I-153	9./JG 52	Map Square 95 581
126	8/18/1942	16:43	I-153	9./JG 52	Map Square 85 253
127	8/18/1942	16:43	R-5	9./JG 52	Map Square 85 494
128	8/22/1942	13:55	Il-2	9./JG 52	Map Square 30 892
129	8/22/1942	14:03	Yak-1	9./JG 52	Map Square 49 154
130	8/23/1942	7:22	LaGG-3	9./JG 52	Map Square 49 413
131	8/23/1942	7:27	I-180	9./JG 52	Map Square 49 194
132	8/23/1942	13:28	LaGG-3	9./JG 52	Map Square 49 271
133	8/23/1942	13:31	LaGG-3	9./JG 52	Map Square 49 194
134	8/24/1942	9:28	I-180	9./JG 52	Map Square 49 421
135	8/24/1942	9:58	Il-2	9./JG 52	Map Square 49 243
136	8/25/1942	11:51	LaGG-3	9./JG 52	Map Square 49 412
137	8/25/1942	17:27	LaGG-3	9./JG 52	Map Square 49 412
138	8/29/1942	14:22	LaGG-3	9./JG 52	Map Square 59 173
139	8/30/1942	16:52	P-2	9./JG 52	Map Square 49 613
140	8/30/1942	17:07	Il-2	9./JG 52	Map Square 49 361
141	9/2/1942	9:12	P-40	9./JG 52	Map Square 49 362
142	9/2/1942	9:15	Il-2	9./JG 42	Map Square 49 441
143	9/2/1942	13:32	DB-7	9./JG 52	Map Square 59 143
144	9/2/1942	17:12	P-40	9./JG 52	Map Square 49 413
145	9/2/1942	17:15	LaGG-3	9./JG 52	Map Square 49 361
146	9/3/1942	13:48	LaGG-3	9./JG 52	Map Square 40 872
147	9/3/1942	13:51	Yak-1	9./JG 52	Map Square 40 852
148	9/3/1942	17:06	Yak-1	9./JG 52	Map Square 40 471
149	9/3/1942	17:13	Yak-1	9./JG 52	Map Square 49 234
150	9/4/1942	10:12	Yak-1	9./JG 52	Map Square 49 241

Confirmed Kills of Hermann Graf

#	Date	Time	Plane	Unit	Place, Notes
151	9/5/1942	16:50	P-40	9./JG 52	Map Square 46 881
152	9/6/1942	13:21	Yak-1	9./JG 52	Map Square 49 163
153	9/6/1942	13:23	Yak-1	9./JG 52	Map Square 49 124
154	9/6/1942	13:27	Yak-1	9./JG 52	Map Square 40 784
155	9/8/1942	11:28	La-5	9./JG 52	Map Square 49 192
156	9/8/1942	11:29	Il-2	9./JG 52	Map Square 49 194
157	9/8/1942	11:35	La-5	9./JG 52	Map Square 49 253
158	9/9/1942	13:21	La-5	9./JG 52	Map Square 49 412
159	9/9/1942	13:34	La-5	9./JG 52	Map Square 49 444
160	9/9/1942	16:46	LaGG-3	9./JG 52	Map Square 44 461
161	9/10/1942	15:24	La-5	9./JG 52	Map Sq. 49 444, La-5 of 287 IAD, VVS, Stalingrad area
162	9/10/1942	15:35	La-5	9./JG 52	Map Sq. 49 444, La-5 of 287 IAD, VVS, Stalingrad area
163	9/11/1942	15:58	Pe-2	9./JG 52	Map Sq. 40 781, Pe-2 of 270 BAD, VVS, Stalingrad area
164	9/11/1942	16:09	P-40	9./JG 52	Map Sq. 40 884, P-40 of 731 IAP, VVS, Stalingrad area
165	9/12/1942	16:47	I-153	9./JG 52	Map Square 49 412, Stalingrad area
166	9/12/1942	17:13	I-153	9./JG 52	Map Square 49 161, Stalingrad area
167	9/14/1942	8:00	I-16	9./JG 52	Map Square 49 453
168	9/14/1942	8:04	I-16	9./JG 52	Map Square 49 420
169	9/14/1942	8:09	Yak-1	9./JG 52	Map Square 49 411
170	9/15/1942	6:35	I-16	9./JG 52	Map Square 49 423
171	9/15/1942	6:39	I-153	9./JG 52	Map Square 49 453
172	9/15/1942	7:05	LaGG-3	9./JG 52	Map Square 49 272
173	9/16/1942	7:35	Su-2	9./JG 52	Map Square 49 271
174	9/16/1942	7:39	P-40	9./JG 52	Map Square 40 882
175	9/17/1942	8:48	Yak-1	9./JG 52	Map Square 40 782
176	9/17/1942	8:52	Yak-1	9./JG 52	Map Square 40 872
177	9/17/1942	14:36	LaGG-3	9./JG 52	Map Square 59 111
178	9/18/1942	11:37	LaGG-3	9./JG 52	Map Square 49 124
179	9/18/1942	11:59	LaGG-3	9./JG 52	Map Square 49 121
180	9/18/1942	12:12	Il-2	9./JG 52	Map Square 39 134
181	9/20/1942	8:20	LaGG-3	9./JG 52	Map Square 40 764
182	9/21/1942	11:32	Yak-1	9./JG 52	Map Square 49 151
183	9/21/1942	11:40	Yak-1	9./JG 52	Map Square 49 132
184	9/21/1942	16:25	Il-2	9./JG 52	Map Square 49 412
185	9/21/1942	17:02	Yak-1	9./JG 52	Map Square 10 162
186	9/22/1942	11:20	I-16	9./JG 52	Map Square 49 272
187	9/22/1942	16:45	Yak-1	9./JG 52	Map Square 49 261
188	9/23/1942	10:42	Yak-1	9./JG 52	Map Square 49 274
189	9/23/1942	11:03	Il-2	9./JG 52	Map Square 49 201
190	9/23/1942	11:05	LaGG-3	9./JG 52	Map Square 40 792
191	9/23/1942	11:07	LaGG-3	9./JG 52	Map Square 49 764
192	9/23/1942	14:30	Yak-1	9./JG 52	Map Square 49 124
193	9/23/1942	14:31	Su-2	9./JG 52	Map Square 49 138
194	9/23/1942	14:33	Su-2	9./JG 52	Map Square 40 794
195	9/23/1942	16:39	Yak-1	9./JG 52	Map Square 40 782
196	9/23/1942	16:42	Yak-1	9./JG 52	Map Square 40 763
197	9/23/1942	16:55	LaGG-3	9./JG 52	Map Square 49 423
198	9/25/1942	14:41	La-5	9./JG 52	Map Square 59 144
199	9/25/1942	14:46	La-5	9./JG 52	Map Square 49 284
200	9/26/1942	8:57	I-153	9./JG 52	Map Square 49 294
201	9/26/1942	16:42	LaGG-3	9./JG 52	Map Square 49 211
202	9/26/1942	16:58	Yak-1	9./JG 52	Map Square 49 451
203	6/??/1943		Mosquito	Staff JG 50	Groningen
204	9/6/1943	10:50	B-17	Staff JG 50	15 km NE Stuttgart
205	9/6/1943	11:08	B-17	Staff JG 50	S of Black Forest
206	1943-44		4-eng.	Staff JG 11	presumably B-24
207	2/11/1944	11:50	B-17	Staff JG 11	5 km S Celle
208	2/24/1944	13:40	B-24	Staff JG 11	Giessen area
209	3/6/1944		B-24HSS	Staff JG 11	
210	3/8/1944		P-51	Staff JG 11	FA-FE
211	3/29/1944		P-51	Staff JG 11	N of Hannover
212	3/29/1944		P-51	Staff JG 11	Schwarmstedt area

War's End and Imprisonment

Erich Hartmann (1922-1988), the must successful fighter pilot of all nations, began his series of victories as a pilot of JG 52 and was there as a Gruppenkommandeur when the war ended. Hartmann, awarded the 18th Diamonds on August 25, 1944, was able to score 352 kills. With Hermann Graf and the squadron members, he shared the lot of Soviet imprisonment and returned home only in 1955. The picture shows Hartmann and his wingman, Unteroffizier Stumpf, during a mission discussion.

On orders from the Luftwaffe High Command, Hermann Graf and his Group Commander Hartmann were to escape Russian imprisonment and fly to Dortmund to surrender to the Americans. Since this, in their eyes, would have been betrayal of their men, both firmly denied this order and, with their pilots and ground personnel, marched westward on foot. The "Graf Assault Regiment", badly armed and scrounging for food, marched through Bohemia toward Bavaria and finally reached the American lines unharmed. On May 8, 1945, Graf and his men surrendered to U.S. troops near Pisek. The Americans treated the men well. But because of a Soviet-American agreement, the entire squadron was turned over to the Red Army ten days later. Hermann Graf, after the Russians had identified him as the famous German flying hero, was badly mistreated, as was Erich Hartmann.

On December 8, 1945, Hermann Graf was transferred from War Prisoner Camp 150 in Gryazovets to War Prisoner Camp 27 in Krasnogorsk. He arrived there on December 9, 1945. The camp had existed since 1942 and was the largest Soviet prisoner-of-war camp for special prisoners. It could hold 60,000 prisoners in all.

While in Soviet imprisonment, Graf publicly expressed the opinion that the war had been wrong and the SS units had committed atrocities. Graf personally had to watch the shooting of Russian civilians by these units at a Russian airfield. He also said during his imprisonment–badly shaken by the outcome of the war, and what later caused him a great problem–he told his comrades that he would also fly in the Soviet air force, since the German Luftwaffe would never exist again.

This view, after his discharge from imprisonment, led to his exclusion from the Organization of Fighter Pilots and to unjustified suspicions that he had spied for the Soviets and wanted to convert to Communism. Despite this, many of his former comrades and friends remained loyal to him.

Acknowledgments:

The author's special thanks go to Mr. Franzke of UNITEC-Medienvertrieb, who made it possible, through its publication by his firm, to make this documentation available to a broad spectrum of readers, and to his wife and two sons, who did without him in his free time so this book could be written.

Bibliography:

Author's Archives; *Jaegerblatt No. 5/xxxvii* November 1988.

Holl, Hans, *Landesr-Grossband 877,* Rastatt, Pabel Verlag.

Jochim, Berthold K., *Oberst Hermann Graf: 200 Luftsiege in 13 Monaten,* Rastatt, Pabel Verlag.

Obermaier, Ernst, *Die Ritterkreuztraeger der Luftwaffe 1939-1945, Vol. 1 Jagdflieger,* Verlag Dieter Hoffmann.

Schreier, Hans, *JG 52—Das erfolgreichste Jagdgeschwader des II. Weltkriegs,* Kurt Vowinckel Verlag.

Held, Werner, *Die Deutschen Jagdgeschwader im Russlandfeldzug,* Podzun-Pallas-Verlag.

Fraschka, Guenter, *Mit Schwertern und Brillanten,* Universitas.

Text and Research:

Ralf Schumann

Photos:

Ralf Schumann archives, Oberst Hermann Graf (ret.), Hauptmann Alfred Grislawski (ret.), Rudolf Fetzer, and Horst Growe (all deceased).

After the War

On December 25, 1949, meanwhile transferred from Prison Camp 27 to Camp 69 in Frankfurt an der Oder, Hermann Graf returned from imprisonment a human wreck.

The ex-Oberst, with 212 confirmed and 40 unconfirmed aerial victories in 830 missions on the eastern and western fronts, and listed in ninth place among the "best" fighter pilots of all nations, began a period in the years after 1950 in which the personal success of his days as a fighter pilot had only a sentimental value.

He did not find it easy to find a place in civilian life, but in the end he succeeded. The former soccer coach Sepp Herberger and the German Soccer League provided valuable help for him.

On July 21, 1970, Hermann Graf appeared publicly for the first time when he presented to the Military History Museum in Rastatt the rudder from his Me 109 from the Stalingrad period, with the 202 kill markings on it. Until his retirement, the world-famous fighter pilot worked again for the city government in Engen.

Hermann Graf died a few days after his 76th birthday on November 4, 1988, in the town of his birth in Baden. With great participation from the population and his former comrades, the honored citizen of Engen was accompanied to his last resting place.

Meeting after the war: Hermann Graf and Fritz Walter, the honorary leader of the German National Soccer Team. Fritz Walter was team captain of the West German National Team which won the final game of the 1954 World Soccer Championship in Bern. He died on June 17, 2002, at the age of 81.

The rudder of Graf's Me 109 with 202 kill markings. On July 21, 1970, he donated the rudder of his Me 109 from the Stalingrad days to the Director of the Military History Museum in Rastatt.

On November 4, 1988, a few days after his 76th birthday, Hermann Graf died in his home town in Baden-Württemberg.

Wolf-Dietrich Huy (born 1917), bearer of the 83rd Oak Leaves, and Gerhard Ille lay a wreath from the Organization of Fighter Pilots on Hermann Graf's grave.

Hermann's Graf's coffin, richly decorated with flowers, lies in the mourning hall in Engen.

Focke Wulf Fw 190 A (works number 2594) with 202 kill markings on its rudder.

Hermann Graf's Messerschmitt Bf 109 G-5/R5 with 172 + 33 kill markings on the rudder. Graphics: Manfred Meier

Emblem of the 9th Staffel "Karaya Squad"

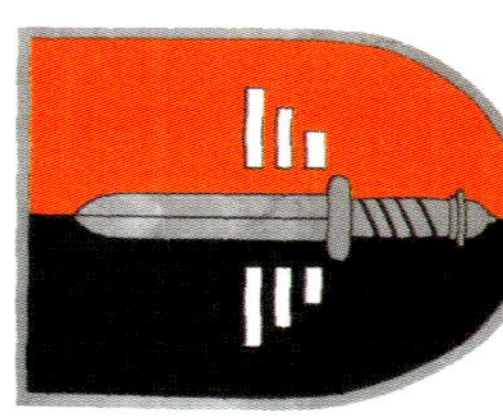

Emblem of JG 52

Hans-Georg Schierholz

A Radioman of the Night Fighters with a Knight's Cross

Decorations:

10/00/1940	Rideau Honors
04/16/1941	Pilot Protection Medal
07/04/1941	Iron Cross II. Class
08/13/1941	Front Flight Badge for Night Fighters in Bronze
05/01/1942	Iron Cross I. Class
07/06/1942	Front Flight Badge for Night Fighters in Silver
08/28/1942	Front Flight Badge for Flyers in Gold
03/20/1944	Cup of Honor for Special Achievement in Air War
03/20/1944	German Cross in Gold
10/29/1944	Knight's Cross of the Iron Cross
11/29/1944	Wounded Medal in Black

Promotions:

03/01/1941	Gefreiter
09/01/1941	Unteroffizier
02/01/1944	Feldwebel
08/18/1944	Oberfeldwebel

Missions:

Approximately 250 missions

Participation in Shooting Down:

57 Night Participations

Foreword

In 1940 Wolfgang Falck, Commander of I. Gruppe of Zerstörergeschwader 1, received an order from Hermann Göring to set up Nachtjagdgeschwader (NJG) 1 and named him Kommodore of this new service arm. Since the strategic bomber offensive of the Royal Air Force began in April 1940 and, because of the heavy losses by day, was now carried out by night, the German Luftwaffe command had to react. Thus destroyer units were gradually restructured into NJGs, and the systematic buildup of the German NJGs took place.

Within a short time, names like Streib, Eckhardt, Herget, Becker, Lent, and later Schnaufer became the basis of night fighters. They achieved great successes fighting the British bomber packs and soon ranked among the aces of their service arm.

But it was not the pilots alone who served decisively in these nightly battles. They flew two-engine planes like the Messerschmitt Bf 110 and Dornier Do 217, and later the Junkers Ju 88 or Heinkel He 219, and their radiomen were on board with them. These specialists guided them to the arriving or departing bomber packs, and directed them, so to speak, to them. Equipped with the most modern technology, they had a vital share in the success of their "coachmen". One of them was Hans-Georg Schierholz, who shared with him in shooting down 44 planes at night, and was able, after Frank's death, to share in another 13 kills with his Gruppenkommandeur, Werner Husemann.

As one of the few radiomen of the night fighters, he was honored with the Knight's Cross in October 1944 for his important share in this success. Thus he was one of only thirteen radiomen of this service arm who received this high honor for their nightly service.

Ralf Schumann

School Days and Training

Hans-Georg Schierholz was born in Lage on the Werra, Lipper Bergland, on August 16, 1921, the son of savings bank director Georg Schierholz and his wife Hermine.

From 1927 to 1931 he attended public school in Lage, moving then to the Realschule in Detmold, where he attained the medium diploma. At the Oberrealschule in Detmold he received his diploma on February 24, 1939.

Schierholz had already begun his glider training on August 15, 1936, finishing by passing an examination on September 10, 1936. Directly after his graduation from school he volunteered for the Luftwaffe. After his application to join the General Göring Regiment in the Luftwaffe had been declined, his application to the Sea Luftwaffe, as the sister force to the Navy was then called, was forwarded.

On March 7, 1939, he was informed by the Command of the Flight Schools and Sea Replacement Department in Warnemünde that he was not suitable for this use, and the acceptance form of December 10, 1938, was declared invalid. The alternative use in the 6th Company of the Air Intelligence Regiment Sea in Lübeck-St. Hubertus could not be done either, since all volunteer school graduate positions were already filled. Thus his application was forwarded to the volunteer equalization position of Air Region Command VI in Münster. But here, too, he was rated as not suitable for use as a pilot or observer, and instead he was entered in the Air Intelligence Troop as a two-year volunteer.

From April 1 to October 25, 1939, he was trained as a workman, finally putting in his Reich Work Service in Department W 60 and working on the building of the West Wall.

On December 1, 1939, Hans-Georg Schierholz was accepted as a recruit in the Intelligence-Radio Replacement Company 18/3 in Berlin-Kladow.

Messerschmitt Bf 110 planes begin a night mission without radar equipment.

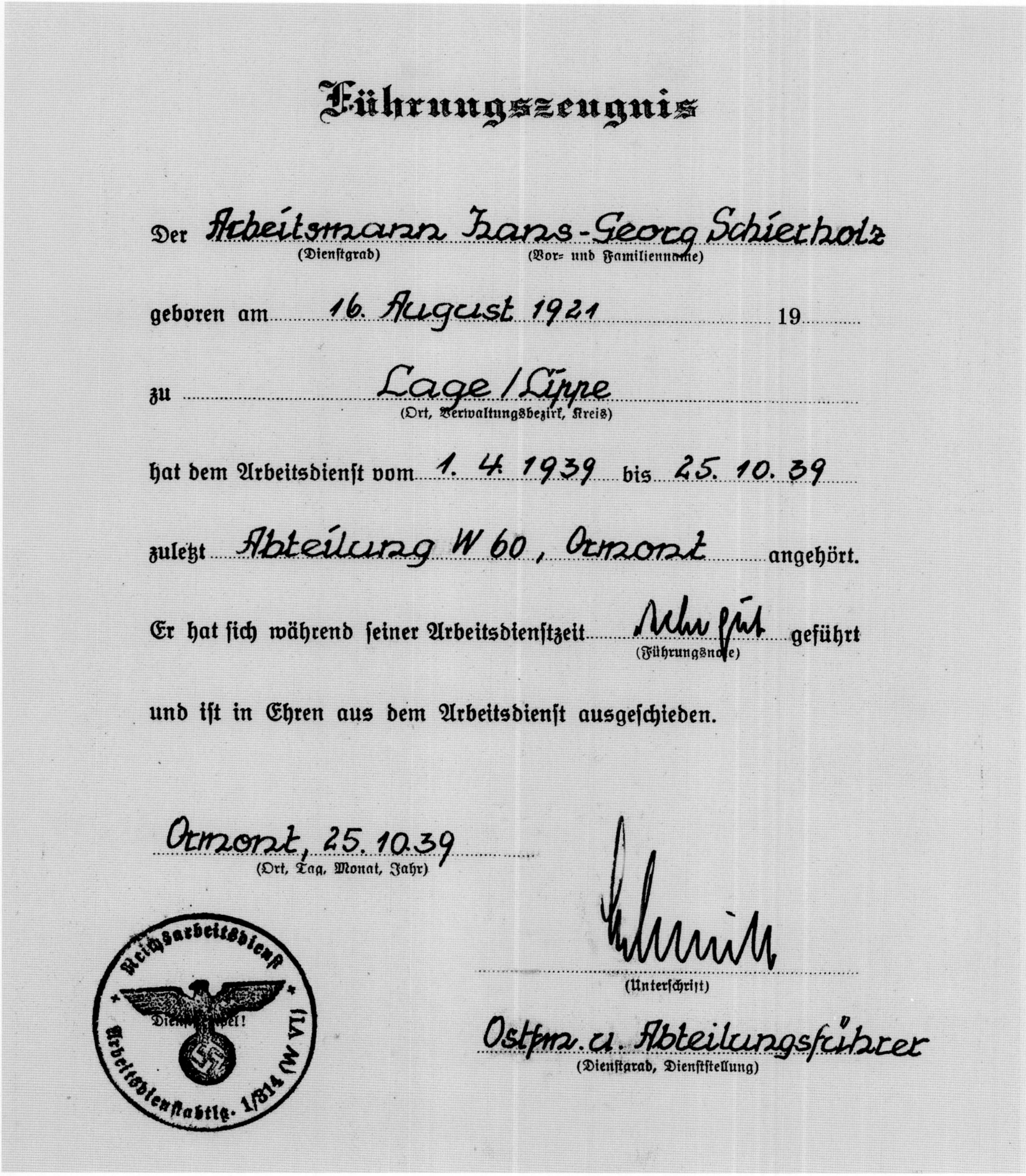

Führungszeugnis

Der Arbeitsmann Hans-Georg Schierholz
(Dienstgrad) (Vor- und Familienname)

geboren am 16. August 1921 19

zu Lage/Lippe
(Ort, Verwaltungsbezirk, Kreis)

hat dem Arbeitsdienst vom 1. 4. 1939 bis 25. 10. 39

zuletzt Abteilung W 60, Ormont angehört.

Er hat sich während seiner Arbeitsdienstzeit sehr gut geführt
(Führungsnote)

und ist in Ehren aus dem Arbeitsdienst ausgeschieden.

Ormont, 25.10.39
(Ort, Tag, Monat, Jahr)

Reichsarbeitsdienst
Dienstsiegel!
Arbeitsdienstabtlg. 1/314 (W VI)

(Unterschrift)

Ostfm. u. Abteilungsführer
(Dienstgrad, Dienststellung)

His certificate from the Reich Work Service, October 25, 1939.

Training as a Radioman (Bordfunker)

On December 1, 1939, he was assigned to the Air Intelligence-Radio Replacement company 18/3 in Berlin/Kladow. On February 27, 1940, he was then transferred to the intelligence office in Neubrandenburg.

He did his aircraft radioman training in the Aircraft Radio School in Halle on the Saale from April 1 to September 13, 1940. After he made his first flight in a Junkers Ju 52 for familiarization on 26 April, Schierholz went to the Blind Flight School in Stargard, Pomerania, on September 14, 1940. He then went to the Destroyer School in Schleissheim on October 16, 1940, to finish his training under the Staffelkapitän, Oberleutnant Specht; it was to conclude on February 4, 1941.

Meanwhile, he had made training flights and was trained in tactical FT traffic, flight security, targeting practice and orientation flights, air gunnery, base flights, and home and enemy navigation for his work as an aircraft radioman.

Hans-Georg Schierholz in full "Star" dress during his training to be a radioman at the Destroyer School in Schleissheim, near Munich. He stands behind the quarters building (winter 1940-41).

Winter 1940-41: During his radioman training at the Destroyer School in Schleissheim, near Munich. Hans-Georg Schierholz (right) with his predecessor with Willinowski, "Coachman" Rudolf Frank.

Stuttgart-Echterdingen, 1941: During night fighter training, Messerschmitt Bf 110s swarm in close-order group flight.

Hans-Georg Schierholz and Oberleutnant Walter Milius at Stuttgart-Echterdingen in 1941.

Stuttgart-Echterdingen, 1941:
Hans-Georg Schierholz in the barracks.

Night fighter training at Stuttgart-Echterdingen in 1941. From left (rear) Blarius, Backhaus, Krause, Brackmann, Hans-Georg Schierholz, Rudolf Frank, Pöschel, (center) Theines, (front) Schlobinski, Spangl, Langer, Oberleutnant Walter Milius, and Thal.

Stuttgart-Echterdingen, 1941: Training on the Messerschmitt Bf 110.

The "Flying Corporals" of 1. (Replacement) Staffel of NJG 3. From left: Spangl, Fast, Schierholz, and Frank.

Transfer to NJG 3

On February 5, 1941, he was transferred to 1. (Replacement) Staffel of NJG 3 in Echterding. Here he flew with the instructor assigned to him, Gefreiter Rudolf Frank, with whom he had already been trained as crewmen at Schleissheim, on further training and drill flights.

On March 1, 1941, Hans-Georg Schierholz was promoted to Gefreiter and the Frank crew was sent to 1st Staffel of 1st Gruppe of NJG 3, under the Staffelkäpitan, Oberleutnant Walter Milius, at the Vechta Auxiliary Airport. On February 16, 1941, after finishing his training he received his radioman's license of the Flight Gunners' Emblem.

On May 9, 1941, the Frank crew took off from Vechta on their first night mission with a Messerschmitt Me 110 (L1+GH). But several weeks were to pass before the first night victory resulted.

On July 4, 1941, the crew took off from Oldenburg at 10:45 P.M. At 12:54 A.M. Rudolf Frank shot down a British "Wellington". For this first night victory participation Hans-Georg Schierholz, along with Rudolf Frank for his first night kill, was awarded the Iron Cross 2nd Class on July 4, 1941.

Just eleven days later they shot down a Handley-Page "Halifax" at 1:05 A.M. for their second kill, but it was not attributed to them, but rather to anti-aircraft fire.

As of August 13, 1941, Schierholz and his pilot had carried out 20 night missions, for which he was awarded the Front Flight Medal in bronze and promoted to NCO effective September 1, 1941. But it was not until the beginning of 1942 that they were able to shoot down another enemy plane.

On January 21, 1942, at 9:03 P.M., they were able to shoot down a Handley-Page "Hampden" northeast of Lingen, and five days later they downed an Armstrong "Whitley V" west of Quakenbrück at 8:36 P.M.

On May 1, 1942, he was awarded the Iron Cross 1st Class. Just two months later, on July 6, 1942, Schierholz received the Front Flight Medal in silver for sixty night missions.

On March 1, 1941, Hans-Georg Schierholz was promoted to Corporal, and the trained crew was transferred as the 1st Gruppe of NJG 3 at Vechta airfield, under the command of Staffelkäpitan, Oberleutnant Walter Milius (left).

On June 30, 1942, at 1:29 A.M., the Frank crew took off from Vechta to attack approaching bombers. On this mission Schierholz had to jump out with a parachute for the first time after the plane had been hit by enemy fire at 2:40 A.M. and both radiators were destroyed.

On July 3, 1942, they took off at 12:41 A.M. from the Vechta field again for an "S" in the Bremen area. Here for the first time they succeeded in shooting down two bombers in one light. At 1:45 A.M. Rudolf Frank shot down a "Wellington" north of Cloppenburg, and at 2:13 A.M. another "Wellington" south of Vechta.

On July 28, 1942, the group had been transferred to Rheine in Westphalia, and the Frank-Schierholz crew flew further missions with a Dornier Do 217 J (D5+GH). With this new type of plane they took off from Rheine at 2:05 A.M. on September 14, 1942, for the Osnabrück area, where enemy bomber packs were expected. They were able to pick up a bomber pack and attack a "Wellington" bomber. At 1:45 A.M. this plane crashed five kilometers east of Lingen on the Ems. This was their seventh kill.

In January, again stationed in Vechta and now equipped with an Me 110 C2 (D5+BH), they were able to shoot down a "Short Stirling" south of Delmenhorst on March 3, 1942, as their fifth aerial victory.

Schierholz and his crew were transferred on April 1, 1943, to 2nd Staffel of NJG 3, commanded by Hauptmann Becker, in Wittmundhaven, and introduced to the Junkers Ju 88 6C. The missions they flew, though, gained no success.

Verleihungsurkunde

Ich verleihe dem

Gefreiten Hans-Georg Schierholz

das Abzeichen für

Fliegerschützen

Berlin, den 16. April 1941

Der Reichsminister der Luftfahrt
und Oberbefehlshaber der Luftwaffe
I. A.:
Der Chef des Luftwaffenpersonalamts

Nr. 74356/41

Generalleutnant

On April 16, 1941, Schierholz was awarded the Aircraft Gunner Medal.

Corporals Schierholz, Frank, Fast, and Spangl (left to right) during the celebration of the first kill of the 1st (Replacement) Staffel of NJG 3 by the Schmolinski-Spangl crew at the end of May 1941.

Meanwhile, the group had transferred to Gilze-Rijen and been equipped with Me 110 G4 planes. The Frank-Schierholz crew was assigned plane D5+CH. By shooting down a "Lancaster" near Antwerp on June 15, 1943, they increased their score of successes. On June 17, 1943, kills 10 to 12 took place in one night. A "Lancaster" pack was spotted over the Schelde estuary on its way home, and Rudolf Frank was able to shoot down three opponents within 41 minutes. Two more enemies, a "Wellington" on 22 June and a "Halifax" on 4 July, fell victim to their guns north of Antwerp.

Transferred to Juvincourt on 16 July, they flew further missions with the Me 110, but they remained without success.

After the crew, now flying a Ju 88 C6 (D5+EK) as their combat plane out of Wittmundhafen field, scored another double on August 24, 1943, of which only a "Short Stirling" at 12:47 A.M. in the Berlin area was credited to them. Hans-Georg Schierholz was awarded the Front Flight Medal in Gold on August 28, 1943, after 100 night missions.

Schierholz and Frank at Bokern, near Lohne.

Hans-Georg Schierholz in the turning ring of a Machine Gun 15, the defensive armament in the rear turret of the Messerschmitt Bf 110, during shooting practice.

Just three days later, on 31 August, they were able to shoot down two more British bombers, a "Halifax" northwest of Venlo and a "Lancaster" east of Diepholz, in two missions.

By the end of 1943 they had raised their score to 26 night kills. In the night of January 21, 1944, two more planes, a "Lancaster" and a "Wellington", fell victim to their guns.

On February 1, 1944, Schierholz was promoted to Sergeant. After the 6th Staffel of NJG 3 had been changed to the 12th Staffel of NJG 1, the Frank-Schierholz crew was moved to the Staff of NJG 3, commanded by Oberleutnant Helmut Lent (1918-1944), at that time the most successful night fighter and the bearer of the 32nd Oak Leaves to the Knight's Cross of the Iron Cross. Lent was later to become the 15th German soldier and first night fighter to be awarded the Diamonds to the Knight's Cross. He died on October 7, 1944, from the results of a plane crash.

For their first joint night victories Corporals Frank (right) and Schierholz were awarded the Iron Cross 2nd Class on July 4, 1941. The awards were proudly documented in this photo.

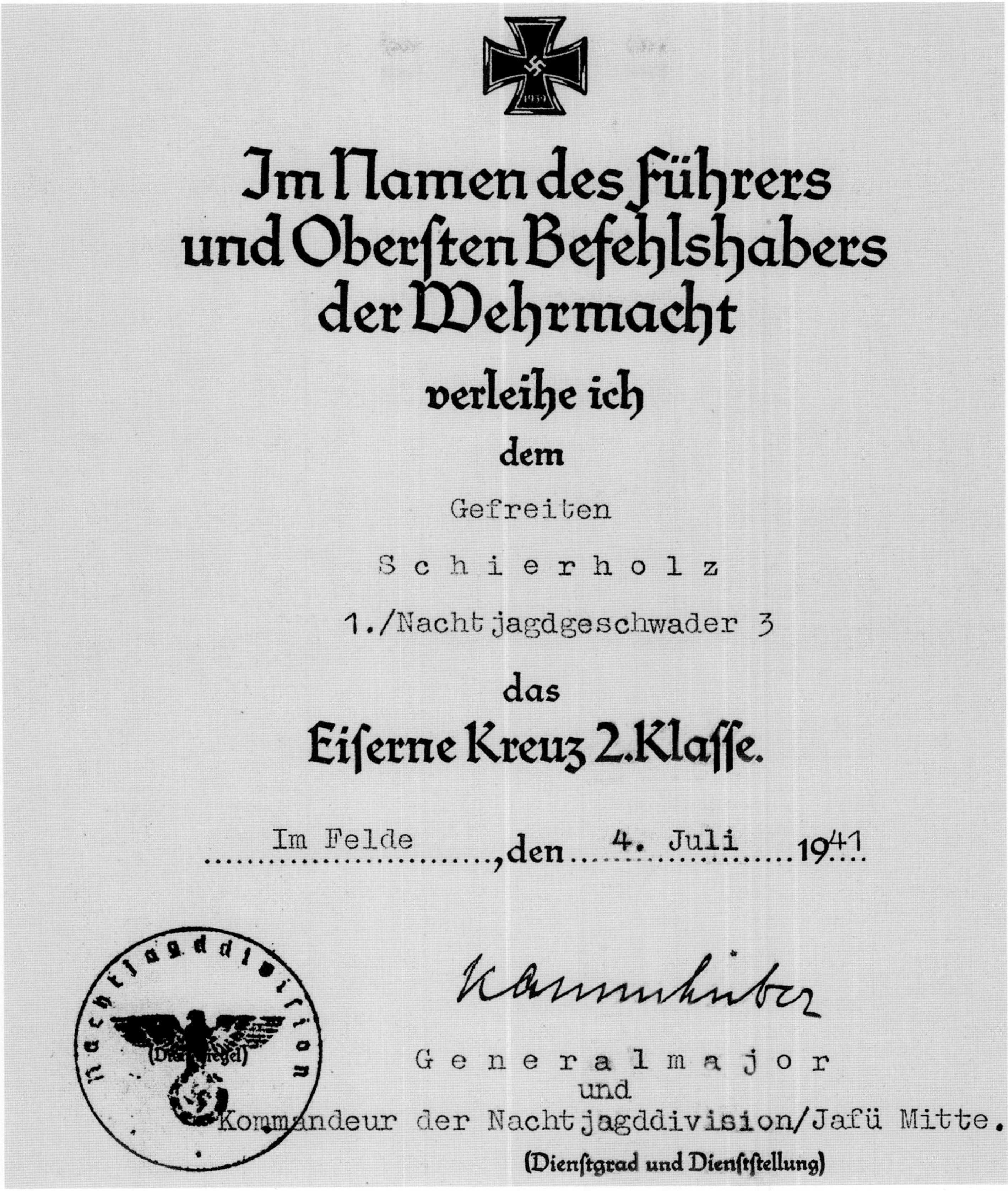

Im Namen des Führers
und Oberſten Befehlshabers
der Wehrmacht

verleihe ich

dem

Gefreiten

S c h i e r h o l z

1./Nachtjagdgeschwader 3

das

Eiſerne Kreuz 2. Klaſſe.

Im Felde, den 4. Juli 1941

(Dienstsiegel)

Kammhuber

G e n e r a l m a j o r
und
Kommandeur der Nachtjagddivision/Jafü Mitte.

(Dienſtgrad und Dienſtſtellung)

The award certificate for the Iron Cross II on July 4, 1941

The Frank crew continued to fly the Me 110 G4 (D5+HL). For taking part in 15 kills, Hans-Georg Schierholz had been honored on March 20, 1944, with the Cup of Honor for special achievement in air war. But since the crew's score had risen so quickly—in the night of February 20, 1944 alone, between 1:53 and 5:04 A.M., they were able to shoot down five Avro "Lancaster" bombers headed for Leipzig, and on the same day the German Cross in Gold was awarded to him for participation in shooting down ten planes. This score went up until March 25, 1944, when they shot down three more enemies in one night, making their total 39.

On 31 March three more enemies, numbers 40 to 42, fell victim to them in one night. On two more missions on 23 March they were able to shoot down a "Halifax" north of Geldern at 2:11 A.M., plus a "Short Stirling" minelayer over the island of Laaland at 11:47 P.M.

On September 1, 1941, Schierholz was promoted to NCO.

Verleihungsurkunde

Im Namen des
Oberbefehlshabers der Luftwaffe

verleihe ich dem

Gefreiter Hans-Georg S c h i e r h o l z

der I./N.J.G. 3

die

Frontflug-Spange für Jäger
in Bronze

im Felde, den 13. August 1941

Major und Geschwaderkommodore

Documentation of the Front Flight Medal for Fighters in Bronze of August 13, 1941.

The Airplane Pilot

Rudolf Frank, with whom Hans-Georg Schierholz formed a team during his training time, was born in Karlsruhe-Grünwinkel on August 19, 1920. In the spring of 1941, as a Gefreiter, he came with Schierholz to NJG 3. At first the space to be defended offered few opportunities for success, and by the end of 1942 Frank had scored only seven kills. This changed suddenly as of the summer of 1943. On August 9, 1943, he received the Cup of Honor for special achievement in air war, followed on October 17, 1943, by the German Cross in Gold. By the end of 1943 his score had already risen to 26 kills.

On one mission in a Ju 88 C6 (D5+HP) against bombers in the Berlin area on December 24, 1943, the crew was shot down over Berlin by a British long-range night fighter and had to parachute out. This incident, for which God must have sent a special angel to protect them on Christmas Eve, remained without further results for the crew.

On April 6, 1944, after the score had risen to 42 opponents shot down, Rudolf Frank was honored with the Knight's Cross of the Iron Cross. Hans-Georg Schierholz had played an important role in this success, as had their aide, Sergeant Heinz Schneider.

With I./NJG 3: Rudolf Frank is at right and Hans-Georg Schierholz is beside him with other crewmen.

The right engine and running gear of a "Wellington" that was shot down on June 26, 1942, by the crew of Feldwebel Stehling and Unteroffizier Hegemann of I./NJG 3 which fell near their field.

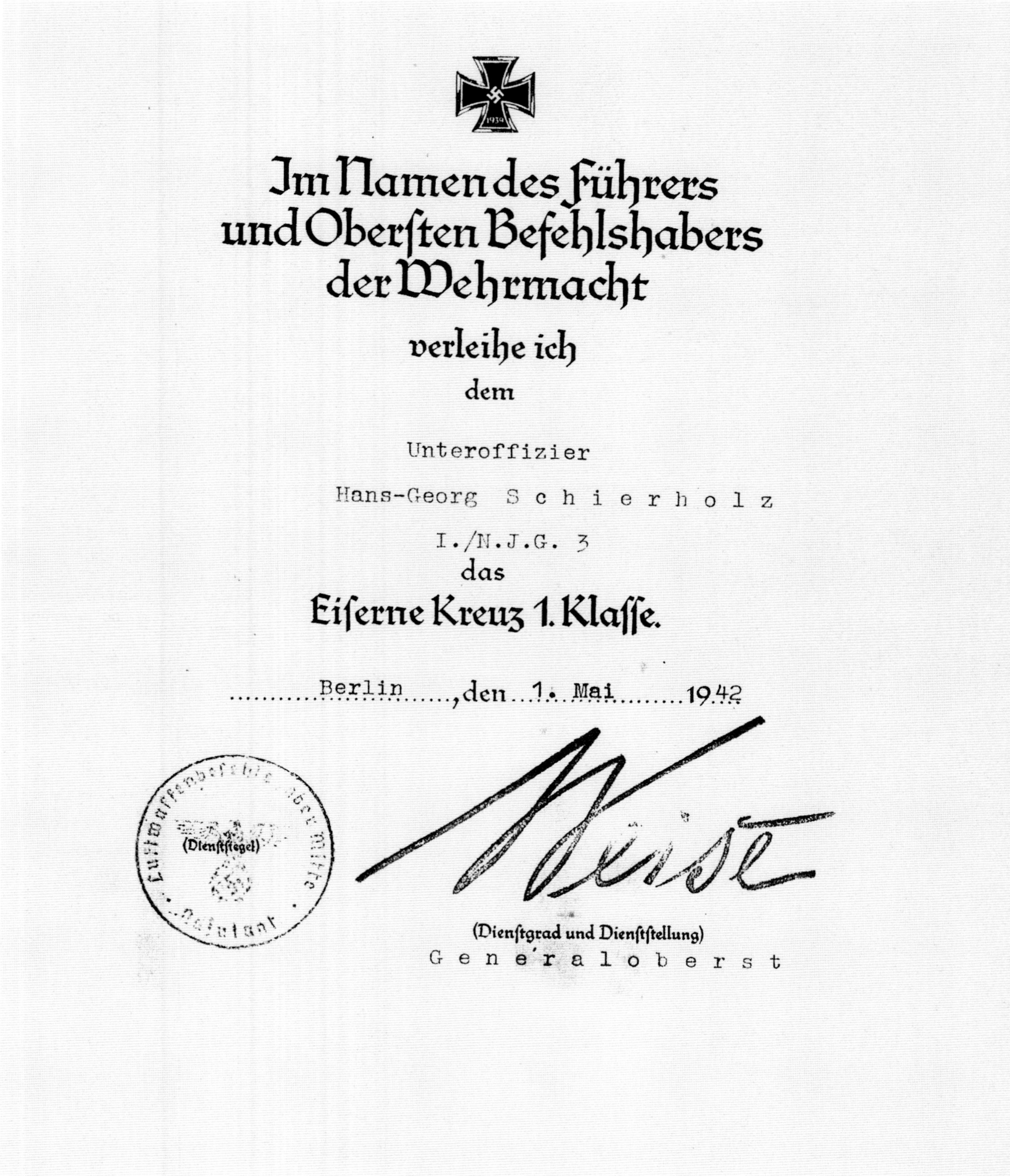

Im Namen des Führers
und Obersten Befehlshabers
der Wehrmacht

verleihe ich
dem

Unteroffizier

Hans-Georg S c h i e r h o l z

I./N.J.G. 3

das

Eiserne Kreuz 1. Klasse.

..........Berlin......,den ..1. Mai........1942

(Dienstsiegel)

(Dienstgrad und Dienststellung)

G e n e r a l o b e r s t

Document of award for the Iron Cross I on May 1, 1942.

For participation in four kills, Hans-Georg Schierholz was honored with the Iron Cross 1st Class on May 1, 1942.

On the night of April 26-27, 1944, the Frank-Schierholz crew took off from Vechta field for a new mission against returning bombers that had attacked Essen. The Messerschmitt Bf 110 G4 with works number 720074 and registration D5+CL was hit by wreckage from a "Lancaster" that Rudolf Frank had shot down (his 45th aerial victory) which caused them to crash. Hans-Georg Schierholz and Feldwebel Heinz Schneider were able to parachute out and save themselves, but Oberfeldwebel Rudolf Frank met his death in the crash of the plane. As the 531st Wehrmacht soldier, he was posthumously awarded the Oak Leaves to the Knight's Cross and promoted to Leutnant. In all, Rudolf Frank had flown 183 missions and shot down 45 planes at night.

On October 1, 1944, the aide, Feldwebel Heinz Schneider, was honored for his share of Rudolf Frank's success with the German Cross in gold, after having been awarded the Cup of Honor for special achievement in air war.

But it was not only the loss of experienced crews that increased steadily; the loss of planes led more and more to the squadrons not being able to maintain their full combat strength. Slow supplying was also a problem, involving both materials and experienced personnel, the latter being hard to replace. The German aircraft industry had suffered much from the destructive attacks of the Allied bomber offensive since the start of 1944. The efforts of the fighter stall in the Ministry of War Production under Armament Minister Albert Speer had nevertheless succeeded in raising the production of fighter planes and night fighters to higher numbers than before. Through the expansion from 27 main factories for aircraft production to almost ten times as many smaller production firms all over the Reich and the occupied areas, the vulnerability of the aircraft industry to Allied air raids had been considerably reduced. But what could the squadrons do with airplanes minus crews, since the production and transport of the planes by day also included further dangers from the ever-increasing Allied air superiority?

Wall paintings in the readiness room at Vechta airfield.

Thus NJG 3 had the following numbers of airplanes to report on May 31, 1944:

The Squadron Staff, equipped with the Ju 88 and Bf 110, reported three planes; I. Gruppe, 23 of 26 Bf 110s; II. Gruppe, only 13 of 37 Ju 88s; III. Gruppe, 20 of 29 Bf 110s; and IV. Gruppe, 21 Bf 110s and Ju 88s of their full strength of 32 planes.

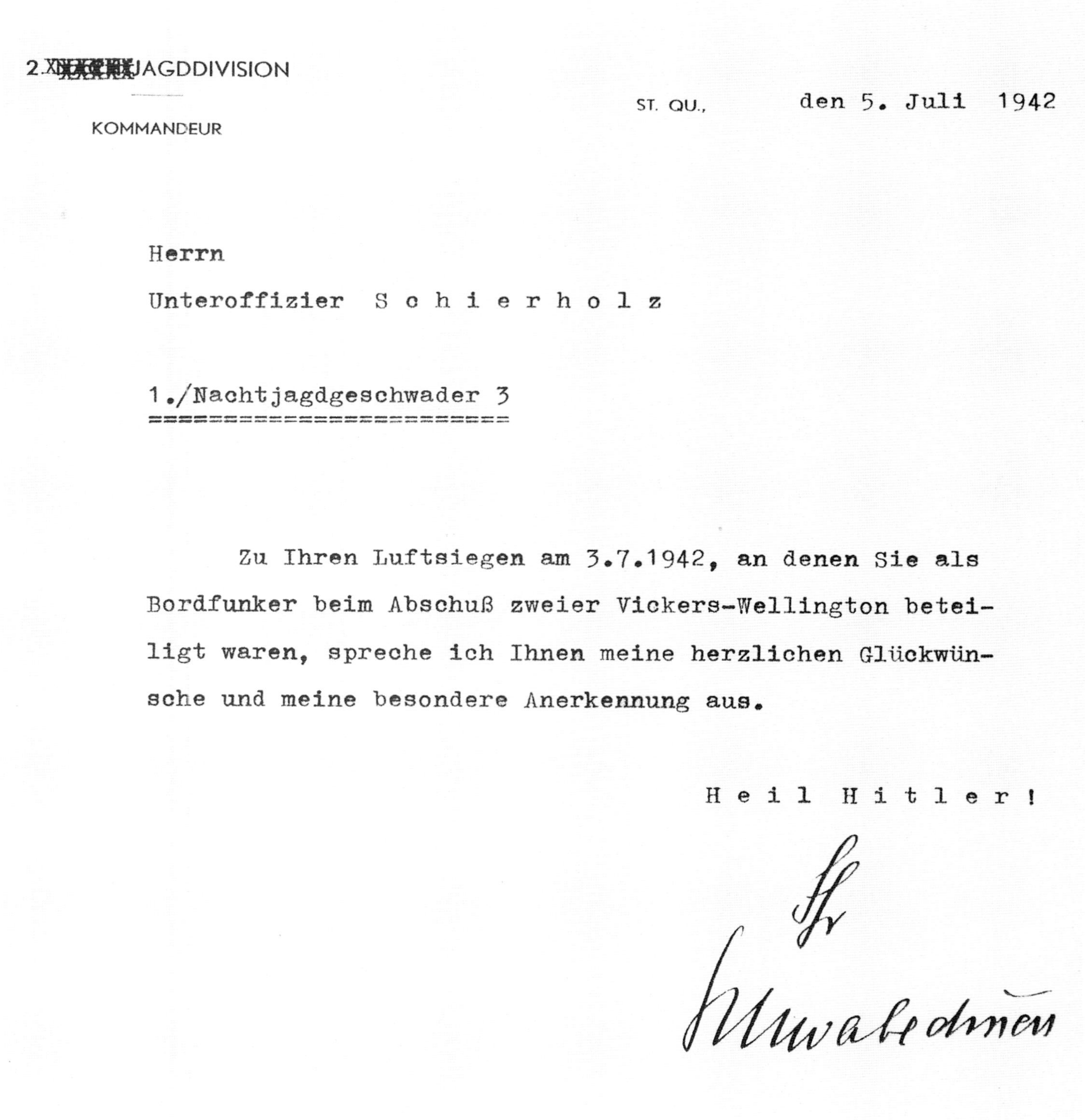

2. JAGDDIVISION

KOMMANDEUR

ST. QU., den 5. Juli 1942

Herrn

Unteroffizier S c h i e r h o l z

1./Nachtjagdgeschwader 3

Zu Ihren Luftsiegen am 3.7.1942, an denen Sie als Bordfunker beim Abschuß zweier Vickers-Wellington beteiligt waren, spreche ich Ihnen meine herzlichen Glückwünsche und meine besondere Anerkennung aus.

H e i l H i t l e r !

Congratulatory letter from the Commander of the 2nd Fighter Division, Generalmajor Schwabendissen, for shooting down two Vickers "Wellingtons" on the night of July 3, 1942.

In the other NJGs it was much the same. The constantly growing stream of bombers, both by day and by night, quickly resulted in more missions and, with the crews trained hastily, to losses that sometimes came on the first or second mission. Even experienced crews with more than 50 or 60 missions and notable kill scores fell victim to the gunners in the bombers, British long-range night fighters, or their own desire to attack. There was also a risk from their own anti-aircraft fire; not rarely were German night fighters shot down by their own flak.

But experienced individual pilots and their crews were able to score success after success despite all hindrances.

Wall paintings in the readiness room at Vechta airfield.

The "Short Stirling", three of which Schierholz took part in shooting down, was the first four-engine Allied bomber and flew night missions against German targets until 1943. Fitted with four 1590 HP Bristol Hercules XI double-star motors, it had a range of 3090 km and could carry 6350 kg of bombs. With a crew of seven or eight men and eight 7.7 mm Browning machine guns, their top speed was 416 kph. Three of these planes were shot down in night action by the Frank/Schierholz crew.

Wall paintings in the readiness room at Vechta airfield.

On June 30, 1942, the Frank/Schierholz crew had to parachute out after they had shot down a "Wellington" and a Handley Page "Halifax" and their own plane's two radiators were destroyed. After their fortunate escape, they are seen in the garden of Night Fighter command Post "3 C" in Emsland.

Verleihungsurkunde

Im Namen des
Oberbefehlshabers der Luftwaffe

verleihe ich dem

Uffz. Hans-Georg S c h i e r h o l z

1./N.J.G.3

die

Frontflug-Spange für Nacht-Jäger
in Silber

Dienststelle
Feldpost-Nr. L 29759

Gefechtsstand, den 6.7. 1942

Schalk

Oberst und Geschwaderkommodore

Award certificate for the Front Flight Medal in silver on July 6, 1942.

Opposite: British Handley Page "Halifax" bombers, here of Mark II Series I, which reached the Bomber Command gradually from 1940 on and flew night missions over Germany and France. These four-engine planes could carry a bomb load of 5900 kg and had crews of seven men. Schierholz took part in shooting down nine bombers of this type. After an attack on such a plane, the crew had to parachute out after the tail gunner of the "Halifax" had destroyed both of their radiators.

Here they are with the Chief Fighter Officer of Region "3 C".

A British Armstrong Whitworth "Whitley" bomber. Planes of this type, fitted with two Rolls-Royce Merlin X V-12-cylinder engines, were in action from 1939 to 1944 and were the first bombers to fly over Berlin. They had a five-man crew and a range of 2400 km. Armed with five 7.7 mm machine guns, the "Whitley" could carry a 3018 kg bomb load. Among the planes that Hans-Georg Schierholz took part in shooting down was a "Whitley".

On the return with "luggage" from Emsland to Vechta airfield. At right is Hans-Georg Schierholz, at left Rudolf Frank.

Oberfeldwebel Gerhard Scheibe (1917-1944) was the first radioman of the night fighters to be honored with the Knight's Cross. He received this high honor on December 10, 1943, after taking part in shooting down 59 enemy planes. Scheibe lost his life on January 22, 1944, after taking part in 65 kills, along with his pilot, Oak Leaves wearer Manfred Meurer (born 1919), when their plane was hit by the wreckage of an already shot-down bomber.

The Avro "Lancaster", here a Mark II, reached the troops early in 1942 and flew its first air raid that March. With a range of 2660 km and a bomb load of up to 6350 kg, the "Lancaster" was the most famous bomber of the British Bomber Command. On the night of May 17, 1943, "Lancasters" flew raids on, among others, the Moehne, Eder, and Sorpe dams, and later destroyed them. On November 12, 1944, "Lancaster" bombers sank the German battleship Tirpitz in the Tromso Fjord. Fitted with four Rolls-Royce Merlin 12-cylinder motors, the "Lancaster" reached a top speed of 460 kph. Armed with ten Browning 303 machine guns and with a seven-man crew, these planes, 7374 of which were built, ranked among the usual bombers over Germany by night. Hans-Georg Schierholz took part in shooting down 31 of this type with pilots Frank and Husemann.

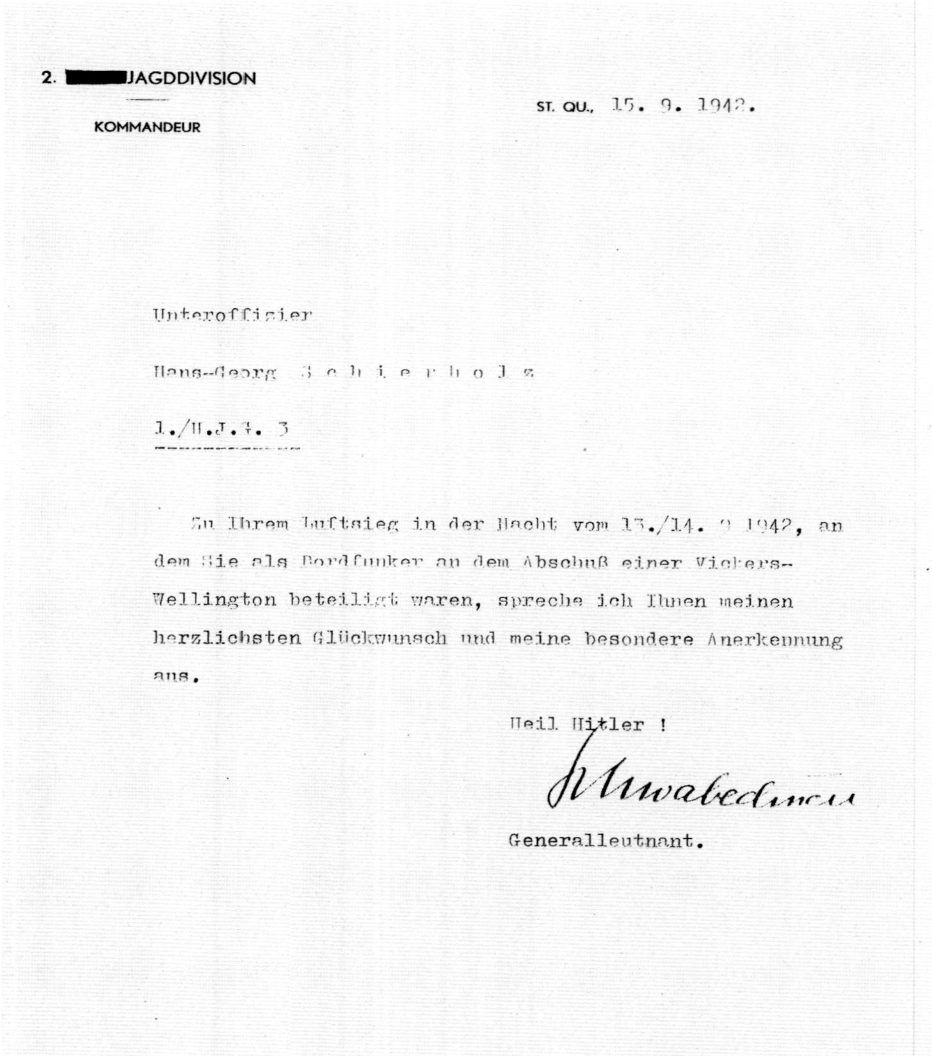

2. [redacted] JAGDDIVISION

KOMMANDEUR

ST. QU., 15. 9. 1942.

Unteroffizier

Hans-Georg S c h i e r h o l z

1./N.J.G. 3

Zu Ihrem Luftsieg in der Nacht vom 13./14. 9. 1942, an dem Sie als Bordfunker an dem Abschuß einer Vickers-Wellington beteiligt waren, spreche ich Ihnen meinen herzlichsten Glückwunsch und meine besondere Anerkennung aus.

Heil Hitler !

Schwabedissen

Generalleutnant.

Congratulatory letter of September 15, 1942, from the commander of the 2nd Fighter Division, Generalleutnant Schwabendissen, for taking part in a night mission against a Vickers "Wellington" on the night of September 13-14, 1942.

June 1943: Gathering of the most successful night-fighter crews in the west. The crews, including that of Frank and Schierholz, have arrived in Gilze-Rijen, Holland.

June 1943, Gilze-Rijen, Holland, with his pilot Rudolf Frank.

A British Handley-Page "Halifax" bomber is prepared by aircraft mechanics and bomb personnel for a night raid over Germany.

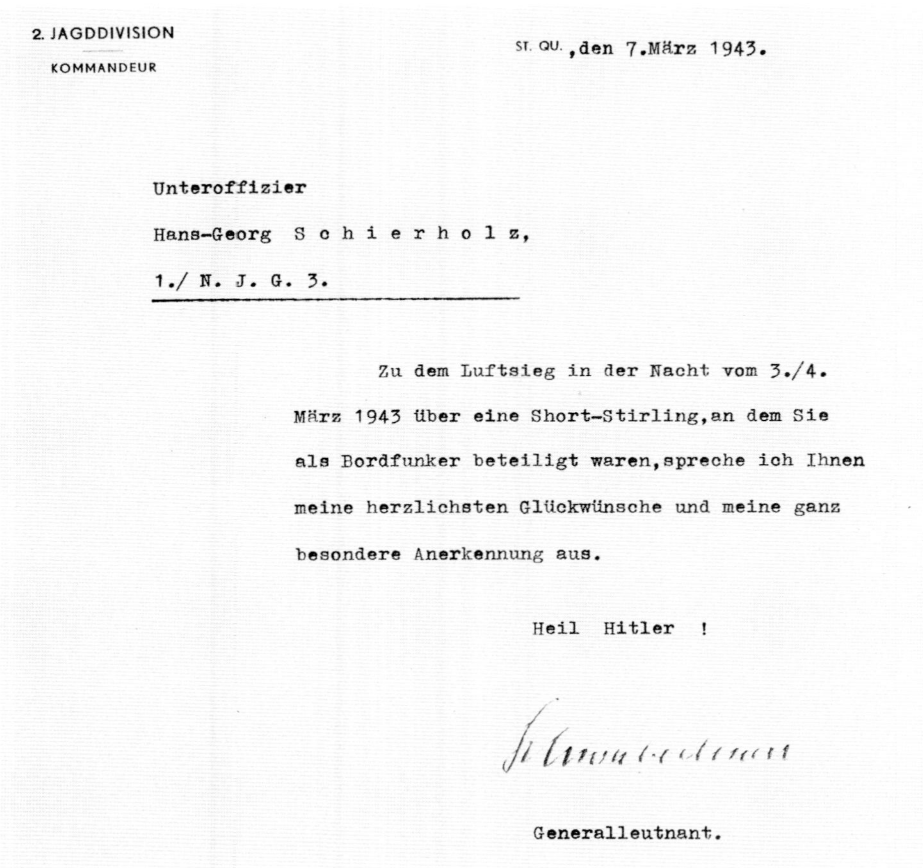

2. JAGDDIVISION
KOMMANDEUR

St. Qu., den 7. März 1943.

Unteroffizier
Hans-Georg S c h i e r h o l z,
1./ N. J. G. 3.

Zu dem Luftsieg in der Nacht vom 3./4. März 1943 über eine Short-Stirling, an dem Sie als Bordfunker beteiligt waren, spreche ich Ihnen meine herzlichsten Glückwünsche und meine ganz besondere Anerkennung aus.

Heil Hitler !

Generalleutnant.

Congratulatory letter from the Kommandeur of the 2nd Fighter Division, Generalleutnant Schwabendissen, on March 7, 1943, for participation in shooting down a "Short Stirling" on the night of March 3-4, 1943.

Streib congratulates Hans-Georg Schierholz on his success to date.

Colonel Werner Streib (1911-1986), as Kommodore of NJG 1, visits the "night fighter experts" in June 1943. Streib was the 54th Wehrmacht recipient of the Swords to the Oak Leaves on March 11, 1944, after shooting down 67 enemy planes at night. From March 1944 to the war's end he was Inspector of the Night Fighters.

Verleihungsurkunde

Im Namen des
Oberbefehlshabers der Luftwaffe

verleihe ich dem

Uffz. Hans-Georg Schierholz

2./N.J.G. 3

die

Frontflug-Spange für Nacht-Jäger
in Gold

Gefechtsstand den 28. 8. 1943

Major und Geschwaderkommodore
m.d.F.d.G.b.

Award letter for the Front Flight Medal for Night Fighters in Gold of August 28, 1943.

In July 1943, the RAF began to use so-called "window" in a series of overwhelming attacks on Hamburg. These were billions of small strips of reflective metal foil tuned to the wave length of the German C-1 radar. The night fighters were disturbed by them, which resulted in a decrease of success in shooting down opponents. Afterward the Bf 110 G-4b was fitted with the Lichtenstein SN-2, which switched out these disturbances by means of a different wave length.

On October 17, 1943, Rudolf Frank received the German Cross in Gold. By the end of 1943 he had raised his score, shooting down 26 opponents at night.

British Vickers Armstrong "Wellington" Mark IC. Used for night attacks as of September 1939, the "Wellington" ranked among World War II's most remarkable aircraft. Fitted with two 1585 HP Bristol Hercules VI double-star motors that gave it a top speed of 408 kph, the "Wellington" could absorb enormous shot damage thanks to its geodetic structure. With a six-man crew, it carried a bomb load of up to 2720 kg. "Wellington" bombers flew the first air raids of the war against Wilhelmshaven on September 4, 1939. From September 1939 to the advent of the heavy bomber, it was the RAF's most important night bomber. Hans-Georg Schierholz took part in shooting down eight "Wellingtons".

A "Wellington" bomber shot down near Wilhelmshaven is raised from the North Sea by a floating crane.

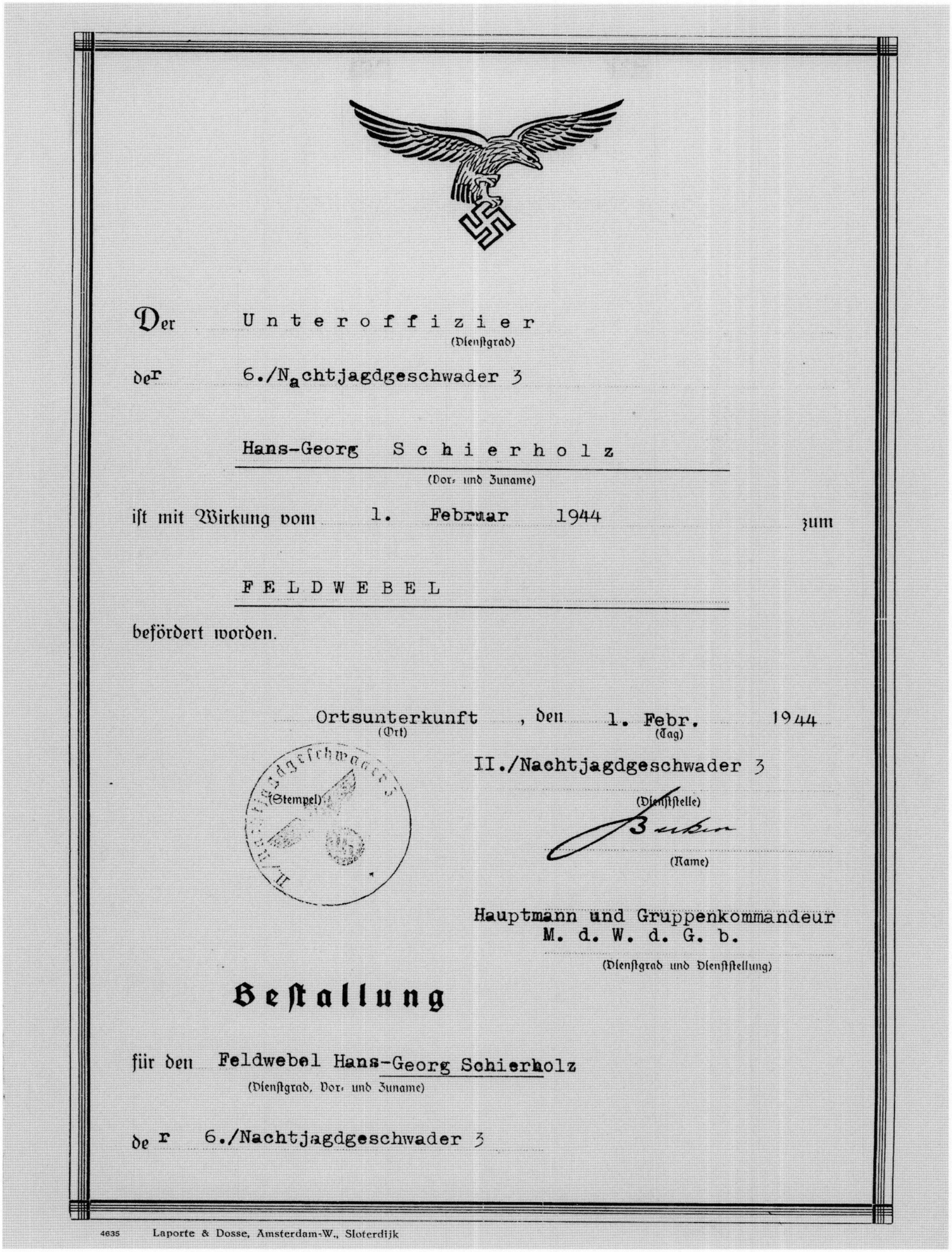

Der Unteroffizier
(Dienstgrad)

der 6./Nachtjagdgeschwader 3

Hans-Georg Schierholz
(Vor- und Zuname)

ist mit Wirkung vom 1. Februar 1944 zum

FELDWEBEL

befördert worden.

Ortsunterkunft, den 1. Febr. 1944
(Ort) (Tag)

(Stempel)

II./Nachtjagdgeschwader 3
(Dienststelle)

Barte
(Name)

Hauptmann und Gruppenkommandeur
M. d. W. d. G. b.
(Dienstgrad und Dienststellung)

Bestallung

für den Feldwebel Hans-Georg Schierholz
(Dienstgrad, Vor- und Zuname)

der 6./Nachtjagdgeschwader 3

4635 Laporte & Dosse, Amsterdam-W., Sloterdijk

Document for the promotion to Feldwebel effective February 1, 1944.

After the 6th Staffel of NJG 3 had become the 12th Staffel of NJG 1, the Frank-Schierholz crew was transferred to the Staff of NJG 3, commanded by Lieutenant Colonel Helmut Lent (1918-1944), the most successful night fighter at that time and the bearer of the 32nd Oak Leaves with Swords to the Knight's Cross of the Iron Cross. Lent was later the 15th member of the German Wehrmacht and first night fighter to be decorated with the Diamonds to the Knight's Cross. He died on October 7, 1944, from the results of a plane crash two days before.

During a mission discussion, Feldwebel Hans-Georg Schierholz holds Frank, the mascot of the crew.

Ich verleihe
dem

Unteroffizier
Hans-Georg S c h i e r h o l z
in Anerkennung seiner hervorragenden Tapferkeit
und der besonderen Erfolge als Nachtjagdflieger

**den Ehrenpokal
für besondere Leistung
im Luftkrieg**

Hauptquartier des Ob. d. L., den 20. März 1944

**Der Reichsminister der Luftfahrt
und Oberbefehlshaber der Luftwaffe**

Reichsmarschall

Die erfolgte Verleihung wird beglaubigt:
Der Chef des Luftwaffenpersonalamts

Generaloberst

The award documentation for the Cup of Honor for special achievement in the air war of March 20, 1944.

An Avro "Lancaster" in flight.

Honored with the German Cross in Gold on March 20, 1944, for taking part in shooting down 25 opponents at night, Schierholz was promoted to Oberfeldwebel on August 18, 1944.

With Rudolf Frank, born in Karlsruhe on August 19, 1920, Schierholz flew as his radioman since his training. Frank received the Knight's Cross on April 6, 1944, at the rank of Obergefreiter.

Generalmajor Walter Schwabendissen (1896-1989) commanded the 2. Night Fighter Division, to which NJG 3 was subordinate, from January to September 1942.

Shot down by a German night fighter, this British bomber plunges burning into the depths.

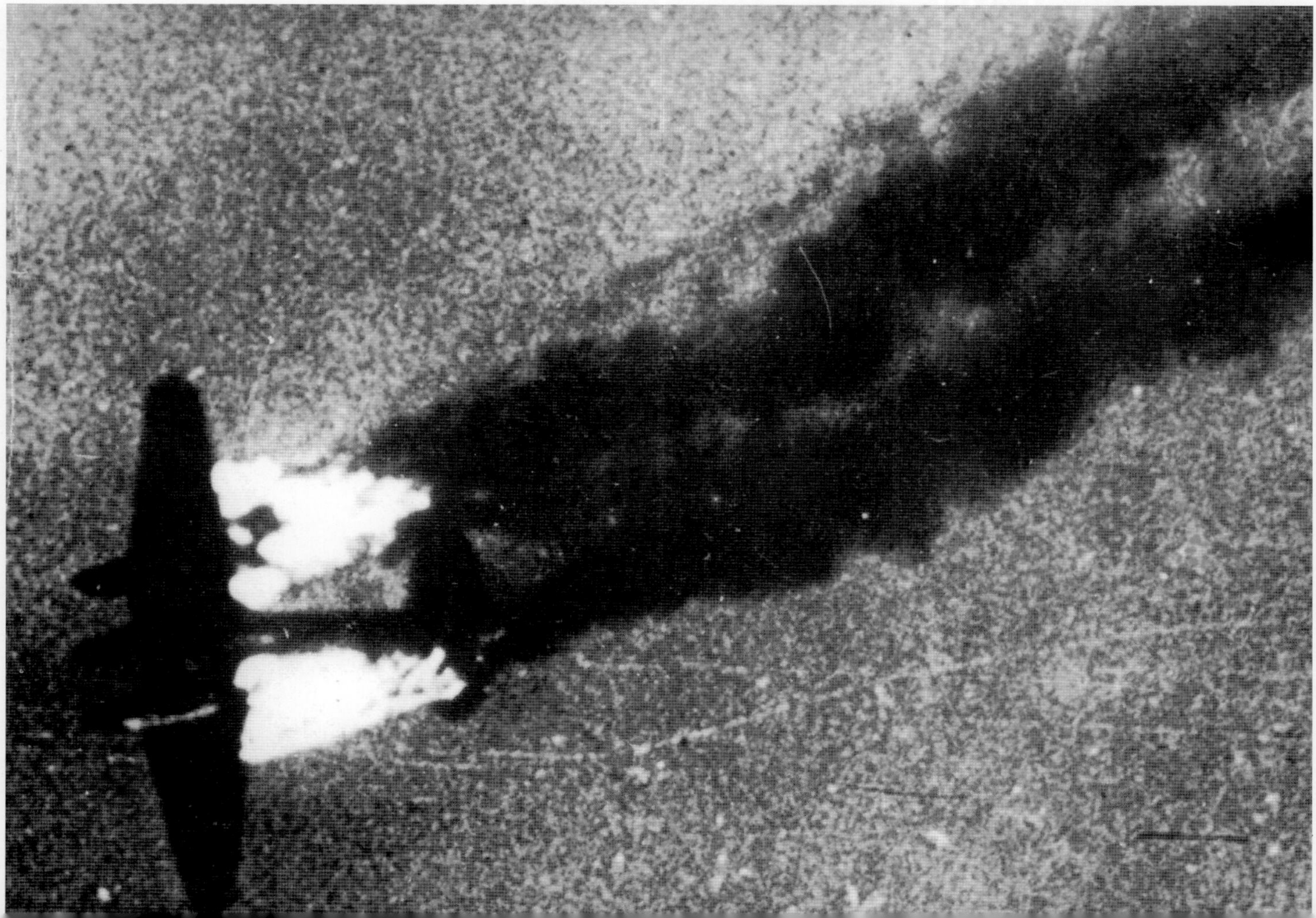

On the night of April 26-27, 1944, the plane of the Frank-Schierholz crew was struck by the debris of an already shot-down "Lancaster". Schierholz and the gunner were able to parachute out, but Oberfeldwebel Rudolf Frank lost his life. He was posthumously honored with the 531st Oak Leaves on July 20, 1944, and promoted to Leutnant.

Hans-Georg Schierholz (left) and Sergeant Heinz Schneider (2nd from right), visibly moved, take leave of their pilot and comrade-in-arms, with whom they were close friends.

Besides Rudolf Franks' parents, Generalmajor Walter Grabmann (1905-1992, right), Commander of the 3rd Fighter Division, also took part in the burial. Behind the parents and the Gruppenkommandeur, Hauptmann Werner Husemann (left), are Frank's crewmen Schierholz and Schneider.

The burial ceremonies for Rudolf Frank.

In the Gruppenkommandeur's Crew

After Rudolf Frank's crash in May 19044, Hans-Georg Schierholz was sent to a spa in Austria. Afterward he flew further missions from the Jagel airfield near Schleswig as of June 18, 1944, with Major Walter Husemann, the commander of I. Gruppe of NJG 3 since January 5, 1944. At first they flew the Me 110 (D5+XB), later only the Ju 88 G6. On August 16, 1944, he was promoted to Oberfeldwebel.

On June 24, 1944, the crew scored its first kill together. Five days later they shot down a four-engine bomber they had attacked; the plane was broken up by 15%. But then the success multiplied. On 5 July a "Lancaster" fell victim to their weapons in France near Calais. On 23 July it was another "Lancaster" that was shot down at 1:34 A.M. over the Ruhr district and added to their mutual score. On the night of 29 July, they took off from Lüneburg on a mission and shot down another "Lancaster" near Hamburg at 1:47 A.M. At 12:47 A.M. on 12 August another "Lancaster" fell to their weapons from the night sky near Braunschweig.

On the night of August 29-30, 1944, the Husemann crew, including second radioman Hein Fehmann and gunner Willi Möller, took off from the Jagel field at 11:20 P.M. heading northward. Guided by the division command post in Stade, Schierholz spotted the first targets by radar over Jutland around midnight. In pursuing one of the targets, the crew found that it was flying from west to east over the southern Kattegat to undarkened and neutral Sweden. Just before it reached the Swedish coast, the Husemann crew came in sight of the target and made it out to be a "Lancaster". They did not pursue it, for their orders were not to leave the German sphere of influence with radar equipment. After they had witnessed several flights into Sweden, Major Husemann asked the division command post for permission to pursue the enemy over Swedish territory. After several inquiries, they received permission via radio around 12:30 A.M. The crew soon spotted a target, which then turned out to be a "Lancaster". In an attack from below, the bomber was shot into flames without defending itself and crashed at 12:48 A.M. in Sweden, east of Halsingborg. A few kilometers into Sweden, they could observe that the enemy airplanes took a southeast course, which they reported to their command post. After further searching they found another "Lancaster", which they also shot down, and which crashed north of Ystad at 1:19 A.M. Since further searching was unsuccessful, the Husemann crew landed at Copenhagen-Kastrup at 1:35 A.M. on 30 August. After refueling, they took off from Kastrup at 2:30 A.M. and tried to find enemy planes returning from the attacked Stettin-Königsberg area, but did not succeed. At 4:35 A.M. they landed at their point of departure in Jagel.

Also successful in constant night action in the Husemann crew, Hans-Georg Schierholz was awarded the Knight's Cross after sharing in shooting down 50 planes. On 29 October this high honor was conferred on him.

Werner Husemann, likewise from Lippe, Gruppenkommandeur of I./NJG 3. Schierholz flew with him as a radioman after the death of Rudolf Frank, and together they shot down 12 enemy planes. On September 30, 1944, after 30 night kills, Husemann received the Knight's Cross. He finished the war with 34 night kills and over 250 missions.

His pilot and Gruppenkommandeur, Major Werner Husemann, born in Schötmar, Lippe, on November 10, 1919, had already received this decoration on September 30, 1944, after shooting down 30 opponents. From 1941 to 1942 Husemann flew in a weather observation squad and joined the squadron staff of NJG 1 at the end of 1942. On 24 October he received the German Cross in Gold. Since October 1, 1943, he was Staffelkapitän of the 7th Staffel of this squadron, and since January 5, 1944, he was commander of I. Gruppe of NJG 3. On July 1, 1944, he was promoted to Major. In more than 250 missions as a scout and night fighter pilot, Werner Husemann was able to score 34 kills.

Oberfeldwebel Heinz Schneider, gunner in the Frank crew. He was also able to parachute out after their plane was hit by rubble from an already shot-down "Lancaster".

A Heinkel He 219 "Uhu" night fighter. This model was conceived in 1940 as a long-distance reconnaissance plane, which was rejected and developed further in 1942, especially as a night fighter. In August 1943 series production began. The He 219 had good flying performance and was armed with two 30 mm and four 20 mm guns, plus two 15 mm machine guns. Since this model was also the victim of personal and political disagreements in the Air Ministry, only 268 planes of various models were built. Fitted with two DB 603 G V-12-cylinder motors, the A7 version reached a speed of 665 kph at an altitude of 7000 meters.

For taking part in shooting down 50 planes, 45 of them with Rudolf Frank, Hans-Georg Schierholz, Oberfeldwebel as of August 18, 1944, was decorated with the Knight's Cross of the Iron Cross on October 29, 1944.

A belated celebration for the awarding of the Knight's Cross to Hans-Georg Schierholz. Gruppenkommandeur and pilot Major Husemann brings him congratulations from superior officers and the squadron, as well as the group.

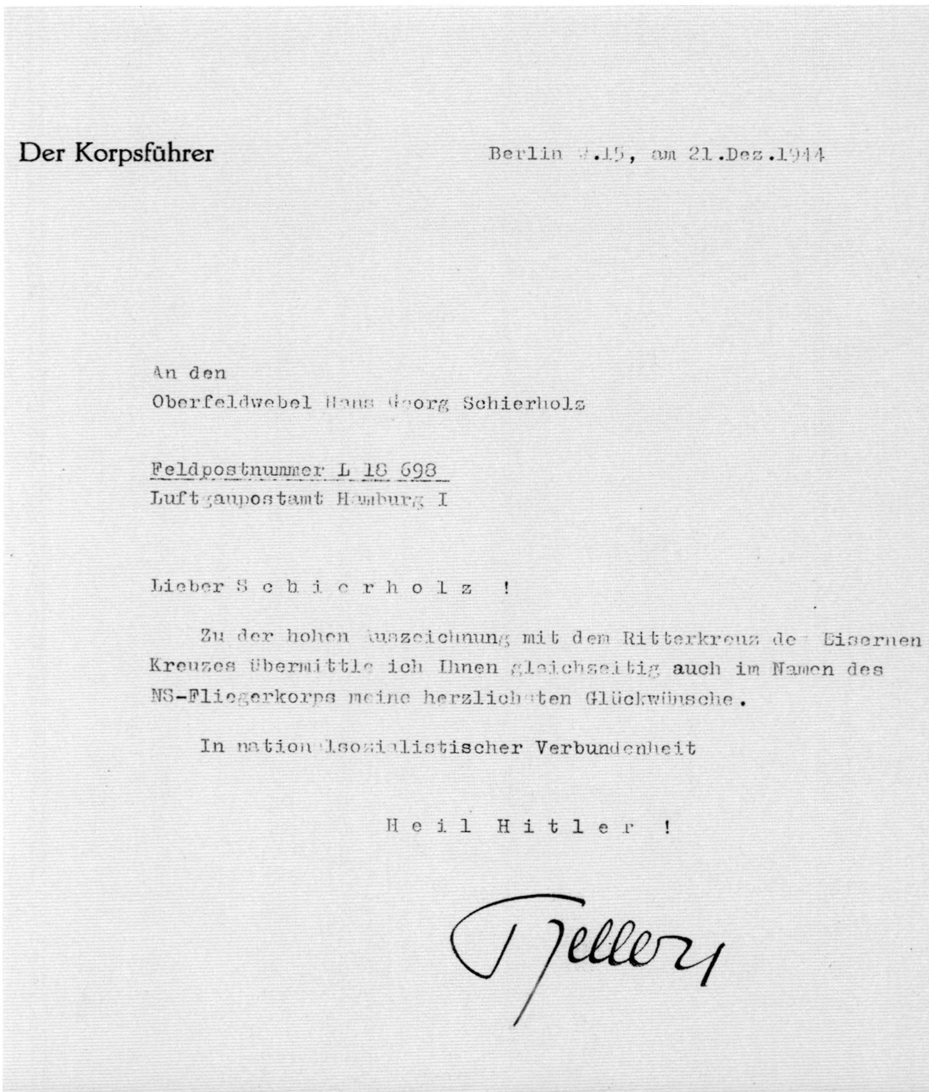

Der Korpsführer Berlin W.15, am 21.Dez.1944

An den
Oberfeldwebel Hans Georg Schierholz

Feldpostnummer L 18 698
Luftgaupostamt Hamburg I

Lieber S c h i e r h o l z !

Zu der hohen Auszeichnung mit dem Ritterkreuz des Eisernen Kreuzes übermittle ich Ihnen gleichzeitig auch im Namen des NS-Fliegerkorps meine herzlichsten Glückwünsche.

In nationalsozialistischer Verbundenheit

H e i l H i t l e r !

The congratulatory letter on the occasion of awarding the Knight's Cross to Hans-Georg Schierholz from Generaloberst Keller, Commander of the NSFK Flying Corps.

On November 11, 1944, the group moved from Jagel to Grove, the former site of a fighter pilot school, in Denmark. Since Hans-Georg Schierholz was on home furlough at the time because of the conferring of his Knight's Cross he followed the group by rail. The group was to remain in Grove until the war ended.

On November 26, 1944, the Husemann crew took off from Grove, Denmark, on a mission to the "Ringelnatter" (ring snake) action area to fight "Agent Providers". There they made contact with a "Short Stirling" at 100-meter altitude over the waters near Assens. During the attack on this bomber in the area between Herning and Grindsted, the Ju 88 G6 (D5+XB) took a shot from the alert tail gunner, who succeeded in destroying both radiators. Both engines failed. Hans-Georg Schierholz was wounded in the upper right leg by splinters from the exploding shot. Because of the low altitude, the crew's last hope was a belly landing in the bright moonlight. Major Husemann was able to land at 11:10 P.M. in the area south of Herning, outside the Grove airfield; the plane was 45% destroyed. Except for Schierholz's wound the crew escaped unharmed. Hans-Georg Schierholz was taken to the hospital in Silkeborg for treatment. For this first and only wound he received the Wound Medal in Black on November 29, 1944. He flew his next mission on February 14, 1945, again from Grove. This time he helped his pilot shoot down two planes. The first crashed on the island of Seeland at 9:17 P.M., the second on the island of Moen at 9:41 P.M.

The new Knight's Cross bearer paces down the honor formation.

Radiomen of the Night Fighters Decorated with the Knight's Cross

Name	Rank	Squadron	Kills	Missions	Born-Died	Awarded
Bundrock, Kurt	Oberfeldwebel	NJG 1	49	130	1917-1998	6/24/1944
Handke, Erich	Oberfekldwebel	NJG 1	59	129	1920-1987	7/27/1944
Heinemann, Anton	Leutnant	NJG 3, 2	56	170	1921-	4/17/1945
Johanssen, Karl-Ludwig	Leutnant	NJG 4, 6	59	68	1921	3/20/1945
Kubisch, Walter	Leutnant	NJG 1, 2	89	300	1918-1944	12/31/1943
Liebherr, Hans	Oberfeldwebel	NJG 1,3,4	68	710	1919-1968	7/27/1944
Nugent, Carlos	FJ-Feldwebel	NJG 2	62	174	1921-2000	4/17/1945
Richter, Johannes	Oberfeldwebel	NJG 2, 5, 100	68	?	1917	9/30/1944
Rumpelhardt, Fritz	Leutnant	NJG 1, 4	100	130	1920	8/8/1944
Scheibe, Gerhard	Oberfeldwebel	NJG 1	65	140	1917-1944	12/10/1943
Schierholz, Hans-Georg	Oberfeldw.	NJG 3	57	250	1921-1996	10/29/1944
Weissflog, Erich	Oberleutnant	NJG 1, 3	48	?	1918-1999	6/24/1944
Wilke, Heinrich	Oberfeldwebel	NJG 2, 3, 5, 100	58	110	1921-1983	11/25/1944

At home in Lage, Lippe on furlough after receiving the Knight's Cross. Hans-Georg Schierholz poses with his mother.

Generalleutnant Josef Schmid (1901-1956) became Commanding General of the XII. Flying Corps on September 15, 1943, succeeding General Josef Kammhuber (1896-1986), and took command of the I. Flying Corps on April 1, 1944. From September 1943 to November 1944 he was Commanding General of the I. Fighter Corps. He was awarded the Knight's Cross as a Generalmajor and Leader of the Battle Group Armored Division "Herman Göring" in Africa on May 21, 1943.

This Dornier Do 217 N-2 of NJG 3 had to make an emergency landing on its own field after taking enemy fire.

A Junkers Ju 88 R-1. This plane (works number 360043) belonged to 1 I./NJG 3 and is today in the RAF Museum in St. Athan. Its crew, led by Oberleutnant Schmidt as pilot, landed at Dyce, near Aberdeen, on May 9, 1943. From it, the Royal Air Force command was able to acquire precise information about German radar equipment.

Bibliography:

Ralf Schumann Archives
Estate of H.-G. Schierholz, privately owned
Obermaier, Ernst, *Die Ritterkreuztraeger der Luftwaffe, Jagdflieger 1939-45,* Verlag Dieter Hoffmann, 1989.
Hildebrand, K./ F., *Die Generale der Deutschen Luftwaffe 1935-1945,* Biblio-Verlag, 1992.

Photos:
Ralf Schumann Archives
Estate of H.-G. Schierholz.

Text and Research:
Ralf Schumann

Acknowledgments:
The author extends his special thanks to Mrs. Luise Schierholz, who allowed him to examine the estate of her late husband, allowing this book to be written; Mr. Franzke of Unitec, who by publishing the book in his publishing house made this documentation available to a broad spectrum of readers; as well as his wife and two sons, who did without him in his already brief spare time so that this book could be written.

On February 24, 1945, the crew flew a mission against minelayers in the Skaggerak, but without success. Schierholz scored his last share in shooting down a plane on March 3, 1945, when they were deployed against supply planes. At 8:29 P.M. Major Husemann shot down a "Lancaster" east of Aarhus. After that they made only short and unsuccessful missions on March 6, April 22, and May 4, 1945.

After 861 flights that are noted in his flight book, with about 250 missions, 212 of them at night, with participation in 57 kills, 13 of them in the Husemann crew, in which Oberfeldwebel Hans-Georg Husemann had to parachute out four times, the war ended for him at Grove, Denmark, on May 4, 1945. Placed in a prisoner-of-war camp at Elpersbuetteldonn the next day, he was released from imprisonment on June 20, 1945. He returned to his home in Lippe, and on July 18, 1945, he obtained a position as an assistant mason for the Baugeschaeft Schulte in Lage.

He studied construction at the Bauschule Lippe beginning September 16, 1946, and worked after that as a building engineer. Active as a Landesbauoberamtsrat until his retirement, he died on February 12, 1996, in Lippstadt, Nordrhein-Westfalen.

May 1, 1945, in Grove, Denmark. The members of the Husemann crew, from left: Feldwebel Hein Fehmann, Oberfeldwebel Hans-Georg Schierholz, and Feldwebel Willi Möller

May 1, 1945, in Grove, Denmark. The radiomen and gunners of I. Gruppe of NJG 3, "the heap of flying foot-folk", join for a group photo. Seated in the front. three from the right, is Hans-Georg Schierholz.

Participation in Planes Shot Down by Hans-Georg Schierholz

#	Pilot	Plane	Enemy Plane	Date	Time	Location	Area
1	Gefr.Rudolf Frank	Bf 110 C4	Vickers Wellington	7/4/1941	12:54 AM	10 km N Grafeld	NW Germany
2	"	Bf 110 D3	Vickers Wellington	9/15/1941	11:30 PM	NW Meppen	"
3	Unterof. Rudolf Frank	Bf 110 E2	Handley Page Hampden	1/21/1942	3:21 AM	near Berge, N of Lingen	"
4	"	"	Armstrong Whitley	1/26/1942	8:36 PM	W Quakenbrueck	"
5	"	"	Vickers Wellington	7/3/1942	1:45 AM	5 km N Cloppenburg	Bremen
6	"	"	Vickers Wellington	7/3/1942	2:13 AM	20 km SW Vechta	Bremen
7	"	Do 217 J	Vickers Wellington	9/14/1942	3:42 AM	19 km E Lingen	Osnabrueck
8	"	Bf 110 C2	Short Stirling	3/3/1943	10:22 PM	S Delmenhorst	Bremen
9	"	Bf 110 G4	Avro Lancaster	6/15/1943	1:24 AM	Antwerp	Ruhr district
10	"	"	Avro Lancaster	6/17/1943	12:58 AM	Schelde Estuary	Cologne
11	"	"	Avro Lancaster	6/17/1943	1:18 AM	Schelde Estuary	Cologne
12	"	"	Avro Lancaster	6/17/1943	1:39 AM	Schelde Estuary	Cologne
13	"	"	Vickers Wellington	6/22/1943	1:24 AM	20 km E Antwerp	Duisburg
14	"	"	Handley Page Halifax	7/4/1943	1:06 AM	N Antwerp	Cologne
15	"	Ju 88 C6	Short Stirling	8/24/1943	12:47 AM	Berlin	Berlin
16	"	"	Handley Page Halifax	8/31/1943	3:43 AM	NW Venlo	Moenchengladbach
17	"	"	Avro Lancaster	8/31/1943	11:28 PM	E Diepholz	Hannover
18	Feldw. Rudolf Frank	"	4-engine	9/6/1943	12:14 AM	Saarland	Mannheim
19	"	"	Handley Page Halifax	9/22/1943	11:25 PM	Hannover	Hannover
20	"	"	Avro Lancaster	9/23/1943	11:42 PM	Mannheim	Mannheim
21	"	"	Handley Page Halifax	10/3/1943	9:56 PM	NO Bad Zwischenahn	Hannover
22	"	"	Vickers Wellington	10/8/1943	12:16 AM	30 km N Norderney	Minelayer, Deutsche Bucht
23	"	"	Avro Lancaster	11/18/1943	11:12 PM	E Lingen	Berlin
24	"	"	Avro Lancaster	11/26/1943	10:22 PM	W Quakenbrueck	Berlin
25	"	"	Avro Lancaster	11/26/1943	11:30 PM	E Papenburg	Berlin
26	"	"	Avro Lancaster	12/16/1943	9:49 PM	E Duemmer	Berlin
27	"	"	Avro Lancaster	1/21/1944	10:57 PM	Magdeburg	Magdeburg
28	"	"	Vickers Wellington	1/21/1944	11:19 PM	Magdeburg	Magdeburg
29	"	Bf 110 G4	4-engine	2/15/1944	7:58 PM	S Wismar	Berlin
30	"	"	Avro Lancaster	2/20/1944	1:53 AM	NW Delmenhorst	Leipzig
31	"	"	Avro Lancaster	2/20/1944	2:21 AM	S Bremen	Leipzig
32	"	"	Avro Lancaster	2/20/1944	2:48 AM	E Celle	Leipzig
33	"	"	Avro Lancaster	2/20/1944	4:33 AM	W Vechta	Leipzig
34	"	"	Avro Lancaster	2/20/1944	5:04 AM	N Meppen	Leipzig
35	Oberfdw. Rudolf Frank	"	Avro Lancaster	3/22/1944	9:38 PM	N Osnabrueck	Frankfurt am Main
36	"	"	Handley Page Halifax	3/22/1944	9:54 PM	W Guetersloh	Frankfurt am Main
37	"	"	Avro Lancaster	3/25/1944	12:22 AM	E Essen in Oldenburg	Berlin
38	"	"	Avro Lancaster	3/25/1944	12:39 AM	N Quakenbrueck	Berlin
39	"	"	4-engine	3/25/1944	1:04 AM	S Papenburg	Berlin
40	"	"	Avro Lancaster	3/31/1944	12:01 AM	W Vogelsberg	Nuernberg
41	"	"	Avro Lancaster	3/31/1944	12:18 AM	N Fulda	Nuernberg
42	"	"	Handley Page Halifax	3/31/1944	12:57 AM	Rhoen	Nuernberg
43	"	"	Handley Page Halifax	4/23/1944	2:11 AM	N Geldern	Duesseldorf
44	"	"	Short Stirling	4/23/1944	11:47 PM	Laaland Island	Minelayer W Baltic
45	"	"	Avro Lancaster	4/27/1944	1:58 AM	E Eindhoven	Essen
46	Capt. W. Husemann	"	4-engine	6/24/1944	1:15 AM	S Calais Boulogne-	Lille
47	"	Ju 88 R2	Avro Lancaster	7/6/1944	12:17 AM	E Dover	Calais
48	Maj. W. Husemann	Ju 88 G6	Avro Lancaster	7/21/1944	1:34 AM	W Ghent	Ruhr district
49	"	"	Avro Lancaster	7/29/1944	1:47 AM	S Helgoland	Hamburg
50	"	"	Avro Lancaster	8/13/1944	12:47 AM	N Steinhuder Meer	Braunschweig
51	"	"	Avro Lancaster	8/17/1944	12:40 AM	S Amrum Island	Kiel
52	"	"	Avro Lancaster	8/30/1944	12:48 AM	E Halsingborg, Sweden	Koenigsberg
53	"	"	Avro Lancaster	8/30/1944	1:19 AM	N Ystad, Sweden	Koenigsberg
54	"	"	Handley Page Halifax	2/14/1945	8:41 PM	Seeland, Denmark	Seeland, Denmark
55	"	"	Handley Page Halifax	2/14/1945	9:17 PM	Moen, Denmark	Seeland, Denmark
56	"	"	Avro Lancaster	3/3/1945	8:09 PM	E Aarhus, Denmark	Kattegat, Minelayer
57	"	"	Avro Lancaster	4/4/1945	11:32 PM	Bourtanger Moor	Hamburg

May 1945, in Grove, Denmark: The Husemann crew, from left: 1st assistant Meisolle; Radioman Hans-Georg Schierholz; Pilot, Major and Gruppenkommandeur I./NJG 3 Werner Husemann; Mechanic Willi Möller; and 2nd radioman Hein Fehmann.

Oberfeldwebel Hans-Georg Schierholz, who flew some 250 missions as radioman in two crews and took part in shooting down 57 planes by the war's end.

May 1945, Grove, Denmark. The members of I. Gruppe NJG 3 on the day of capitulation. From left: Kurt Ulrich, Sepp Kinnner, ?, H.-G. Schierholz, ?, ?, Hans Paul, ?, ?, ?, ?, Hans Höner, Fritz Hartig, Gruppenkommandeur Knight's Cross Bearer Werner Husemann, ?, Heinz Krause, Richard Mrosik, Willi Möller (Husemann-Schierholz crew), ?, ?, Hein Fehmann (Husemann-Schierholz crew), Heinz Schneider (Frank-Schierholz crew), Heinz Schadowski, ?, Ludwig Fischer, ?, ?, ?, Bernhard Brink, and Maisolle, first aide on the Commander's plane.

A Junkers Ju 88 G night fighter taken by the British in Denmark after the surrender.

August 23, 1987: Hans-Georg Schierholz and Heinz Schneider, former members of Rudolf Frank's crew, at Frank's grave in the military cemetery at Ysselstein, Holland.